C O N T E M P O R A R Y ' S

Breakthroughs

in Social Studies

CONTEMPORARY'S
Breakthroughs
in Social Studies

Developing Reading and Critical Thinking Skills
Kenneth Tamarkin

CONTEMPORARY BOOKS

a division of NTC/CONTEMPORARY PUBLISHING GROUP
Lincolnwood, Illinois USA

ISBN: 0-8092-3285-5

Published by Contemporary Books,
a division of NTC/Contemporary Publishing Group, Inc.,
4255 West Touhy Avenue,
Lincolnwood (Chicago), Illinois 60712-1975 U.S.A.

Consultants/Field Testers
Sr. Kathleen Bahlinger, C.S.J.
Sr. Lory Schaff, C.S.J.

Director New Product Development
Noreen Lopez

Editorial Manager
Cynthia Krejcsi

Executive Editor
Marilyn Cunningham

Project Editors
Joan Conover
Christine Kelner

Design and Production Manager
Thomas D. Scharf

Cover Design
Michael Kelly

Interior Illustrations
David Will

Cover Images
Image Bank; Stock Imagery

CONTENTS

ACKNOWLEDGMENTS

Cartoon on page 3 by Peter Oakley, Modern Wonder Cartoons, America OnLine. Copyright 1994 by Peter Oakley. Reprinted by permission.

Excerpt on page 18 from *A People's History of the United States* by Howard Zinn. Copyright 1980 by Howard Zinn. Reprinted by permission of HarperCollins Publishers.

Excerpts on pages 27 and 28 from *The Black Americans: A History in Their Own Words*, edited by Milton Meltzer. Copyright 1964, 1965, 1967, 1984 by Milton Meltzer. Reprinted by permission of HarperCollins Publishers.

Excerpt on page 28 from *Let Them Speak for Themselves, Women in the American West,* 1849–1900, edited by Christine Fischer. Copyright 1977 by Archon Books.

Excerpts on pages 42 and 44 from *A People's History of the United States* by Howard Zinn. Copyright 1980 by Howard Zinn. Reprinted by permission of HarperCollins Publishers.

Graph on page 56 copyright © 1986 by The New York Times Company. Reprinted by permission.

Graph on page 67 reprinted courtesy of *The Boston Globe*. Copyright 1986 *The Boston Globe*.

Maps on pages 95, 97, and 107 from *American History Atlas* by Martin Gilbert. Copyright 1968 by Martin Gilbert. Originally published in Great Britain by Weidenfeld and Nicolson, London.

Cartoon on page 122 by Michael Keefe, dePIXion Features, Inc. Copyright 1995 by Michael Keefe. Reprinted by permission.

Cartoon on page 124 by Oliphant. Copyright 1967, Universal Press Syndicate. Reprinted by permission. All rights reserved.

Cartoon on page 126 by Dick Locher. Reprinted by permission of Tribune Media Services.

Excerpt on page 137 from *The American Reader* by Paul Angle. Copyright 1958.

Cartoon on page 139 by Tony Auth. Copyright 1985, *Philadelphia Inquirer*. Reprinted by permission of Universal Press Syndicate. All rights reserved.

Map on page 145 from *American History Atlas* by Martin Gilbert. Copyright 1968 by Martin Gilbert. Originally published in Great Britain by Weidenfeld and Nicolson, London.

Cartoon on page 151 by Don Wright. Copyright 1985 by Don Wright, *The Miami News*.

Cartoon on page 154 by Mike Peters. Copyright 1986 by *Dayton Daily News*. Reprinted by permission of Tribune Media Services.

Cartoon on page 156 by Bruce Beattie. Copyright 1983 by *Daytona Beach Morning Journal*. Reprinted by permission of Copley News Service.

Cartoon on page 167 by Oliphant. Copyright 1986, Universal Press Syndicate. Reprinted by permission. All rights reserved.

Cartoon on page 189 by Michael Keefe, dePIXion Features, Inc. Copyright 1995 by Michael Keefe. Reprinted by permission.

The editors have made every effort to trace the ownership of all copyrighted material, and necessary permissions have been secured in most cases. Should there prove to be any question regarding the use of any material, regret is hereby expressed for such error. Upon notification of any such oversight, proper acknowledgment will be made in future editions.

TO THE INSTRUCTOR

This *Breakthroughs in Social Studies* text is designed to help students develop the critical reading and thinking skills they need to successfully work with social studies materials. Students working in this book receive a thorough grounding in the organization and comprehension of written material and illustrations. Then they are introduced to the higher-order thinking skills—analysis, evaluation, synthesis, and application.

The book emphasizes the step-by-step acquisition of skills rather than discrete knowledge. Materials from the five major social studies areas—history, economics, political science, behavioral science, and geography—are represented throughout the text.

Some special features to note are the pre-test and post-test, the chapter reviews, and the answer key.

- **Pre-Test** and **Post-Test.** These tests are in multiple-choice format, similar to that found on many tests. Questions are drawn from the entire range of skills and content in the book. Evaluation charts correlated to the chapters help you identify strong and weak areas for each student.

- **Chapter Reviews.** These tests, also in multiple-choice format, are brief reviews of the skills taught in the chapter. Evaluation charts help you see which parts of a chapter a student might need to review before moving on.

- **Answer Keys.** A full answer key is located in the back of the text. Students should be encouraged to check their answers as soon as they complete an exercise to ensure that they have mastered the material.

Some exercises in this book ask students to write short answers in their own words. They should make every effort to complete these written exercises, since writing has been shown to be one of the most effective demonstrations of learning and comprehension. When coaching your students in writing tasks, focus on their ideas and how they can be expressed clearly before concentrating on spelling, grammar, or handwriting.

Finally, encourage your students to read and help them find appropriate materials. The short passages in this book are no substitute for the real reading opportunities available to your students. By becoming more comfortable with reading, they will prepare themselves not only for social studies materials but for lifelong learning.

TO THE STUDENT

Welcome to *Breakthroughs in Social Studies*. In this book, you'll learn how to study reading passages as well as illustrations such as charts, graphs, maps, and cartoons.

Before you begin work in this text, take the pre-test. It will help you identify chapters to focus on as you move through the text. When you are finished with the text, the post-test will help you evaluate the work you have done.

You'll find answers to all the exercises at the back of the book. Be sure to check yourself at the end of each exercise before you move on. And when an exercise asks you to write, answer fully in your own words. Writing is a very important part of learning. Don't worry too much about your handwriting or about grammar and spelling. First get your ideas on paper; then reread to improve what you've written.

Finally, read beyond the pages of this book. Read newspapers, magazines, road maps, and anything else you find useful or interesting. Reading will help you prepare not only for social studies materials but also for the rest of your life.

PRE-TEST

This pre-test is a guide to using this book. You should take the pre-test before you start working on any of the chapters. The questions will test the social studies reading and reasoning skills covered in this book.

Directions: Study each passage or illustration, then answer the questions that follow.

Questions 1–3 are based on the following passage.

> The Sultan of Brunei may not control a large nation, but his rule has its rewards. With a fortune worth about $37 billion, Sultan Hassanal Bolkiah is considered the richest man in the world.
>
> His wealth comes from the vast pool of oil lying beneath his small island nation. Thanks to that oil, the sultan is able to give his 369,000 subjects one of the highest standards of living in Asia. No one pays personal income taxes in Brunei, and yet, the government provides a host of social services like free medical care, free primary-school education, and old-age pensions.
>
> 1992 was the sultan's 25th year as king, and many people hoped that he would celebrate by restoring democracy to Brunei. Instead, the sultan simply promised to further increase the standard of living. His pampered subjects didn't complain.

1. A sultan is

    (1) a king
    (2) a rich man
    (3) a pampered subject
    (4) an Arab
    (5) a president

2. What is the form of government of Brunei?

    (1) democracy, rule by the people with free elections
    (2) military dictatorship, rule by the head of the armed forces
    (3) monarchy, rule by a single member of a royal family
    (4) theocracy, rule by priests
    (5) oligarchy, rule by a small elite group

3. What is the main idea of this passage?

    (1) The people of Brunei are involved in decision making and
        planning for the future of the country.
    (2) Brunei is not a very large nation, but the sultan enjoys
        ruling it.
    (3) The wealthy sultan of Brunei keeps control over his people but
        provides for them generously.
    (4) The sultan of Brunei is planning to take over neighboring
        nations in order to enlarge his country.
    (5) The standard of living in Brunei will be improving since the
        sultan celebrated his 25th year on the throne.

Question 4 is based on the following passage.

> As a word-processing teacher, I am often called by companies interested in hiring my students. When they ask for a recommendation, they do not first ask about skills, intelligence, age, or appearance. The first question is almost always about attendance and punctuality.

4. What do companies value most in their word-processing employees?

    (1) potential
    (2) attractiveness
    (3) youth
    (4) dependability
    (5) knowledge

Questions 5–7 are based on the following cartoon.

Background clues: Prison overcrowding in the United States has forced judges to seek alternative ways of punishing people convicted of crimes. Community service, payments to victims, and boot camps are just some of the alternative sentences U.S. judges have used.

"You can take the five years and $60,000 in fines, or you can go for Door Number Two where officer Meryl is standing."

5. Who is the speaker in this cartoon?

   (1) a judge
   (2) a defendant
   (3) a preacher
   (4) a law professor
   (5) a police officer

6. When the cartoonist writes, "You can go for Door Number Two where officer Meryl is standing," he is comparing modern trials to

   (1) birthday parties
   (2) war
   (3) classrooms
   (4) game shows
   (5) horrible ordeals

7. The point of this cartoon is that alternative sentencing

   (1) makes punishment a matter of luck
   (2) helps trials move more smoothly
   (3) is a more humane way of punishing criminals
   (4) discourages potential criminals from committing crimes
   (5) saves the government a lot of money

Questions 8–10 are based on the following passage.

Caroline rushed out to use her brand-new credit card at Sears. She went straight to the home improvement department and bought wallpaper and paint to redecorate the kitchen. She took the supplies to the cashier and handed over her credit card. The cashier made out a sales slip from Caroline's card. After signing the sales slip, Caroline sailed out of the store and immediately started her project.

At the end of the month, Caroline was shocked when she received her statement. She had not realized that the supplies cost so much. The statement listed all her credit purchases and the total amount she owed Sears. She could afford to pay only the minimum payment, not the whole amount she owed. As a result, she had to pay interest to Sears on the unpaid portion.

8. Before she could leave the store with her purchases, Caroline had to
   (1) sign the sales slip
   (2) pay the total amount due with a check
   (3) receive her monthly statement
   (4) leave her credit card with the cashier
   (5) leave a security deposit

9. In which of the following situations would you use a credit card in the same way as Caroline did?
   (1) buying dinner for your family at McDonald's
   (2) renting an apartment from a realtor
   (3) buying new shoes at a shoe store
   (4) placing a mail order by phone
   (5) withdrawing money from an automatic teller machine

10. Caroline had to pay interest to Sears because
    (1) she could not afford to make the minimum payment
    (2) whenever you buy something with a credit card, you have to pay interest
    (3) she could not afford to pay the full amount she owed
    (4) she was so shocked when she received her statement
    (5) the supplies she bought were on sale

Questions 11–12 are based on the following graph.

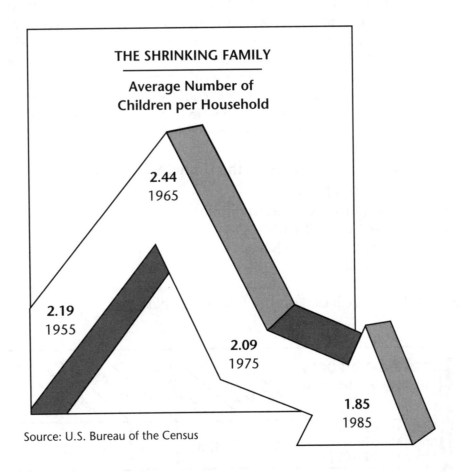

THE SHRINKING FAMILY

**Average Number of
Children per Household**

2.44
1965

2.19
1955

2.09
1975

1.85
1985

Source: U.S. Bureau of the Census

11. In what year did Americans have the greatest number of children per household?

   (1) 1955
   (2) 1965
   (3) 1975
   (4) 1980
   (5) 1985

12. Which of the following is a reasonable conclusion based on this graph?

   (1) American children today generally have fewer brothers and sisters than was the case a generation ago.
   (2) Americans of 1985 were earning more money than they had thirty years before and could therefore better provide for their children.
   (3) As of 1985, there was a growing need for more elementary schools.
   (4) Most Americans are deciding not to have any children because they believe the world is too dangerous a place for a child.
   (5) There has been an increase in single-parent households, resulting in a decline in the average number of children per household.

Question 13 is based on the following passage.

> The United States can be thought of as a land of invention. For example, in the area of transportation, America has been responsible for more progress than any other nation in the world. American firsts include the steamboat, the airplane, and the nuclear submarine. The nineteenth century's most extensive railroad system was built in our country. In addition, the mass production of automobiles began in the United States, and our highway system is the best in the world.

13. In the area of transportation, the United States has
    (1) been a world leader
    (2) concentrated on the automobile
    (3) neglected the railroads
    (4) followed progress in Europe
    (5) resisted change

Questions 14–15 are based on the following chart.

STRATEGIC IMPORTS (Averages in percent)	Platinum group metals	Chromium	Vanadium	Manganese	Gold
Share of U.S. imports originating in South Africa (1990–1993)	47%	43%	13%	24%	NA
South Africa's share of world reserves	89%	60%	50%	92%	26%
South Africa's share of world production (1994)	60%	31%	30%	36%	48%

Sources: U.S. Bureau of Mines; United Nations

14. What percentage of the chromium imported into the United States came from South Africa?
    (1) 13%
    (2) 31%
    (3) 43%
    (4) 47%
    (5) 60%

15. Platinum group metals, chromium, vanadium, and manganese are all important to American industry. What does the chart tell you about the relationship of South Africa to the United States?

    (1) The United States has no relationship with South Africa.
    (2) South Africa relies on the United States for valuable metals.
    (3) The United States could get along easily without imports from South Africa.
    (4) South Africa provides the United States with important raw materials.
    (5) South Africa lacks natural mineral resources.

Questions 16–18 are based on the following passage.

> In May 1607, the first permanent English colony in what is now the United States was founded at Jamestown, Virginia. The colonists built their village on a terrible swamp, and then the men spent their time looking for gold. The entire colony would have starved if not for the help of the native chief Powhatan, who gave the settlers food.
>
> The colony struggled along until John Rolfe discovered the American tobacco plant. Virginia began to export tobacco to Europe, where it became very popular. The success of the Virginia colony was assured.

16. After building their village, the first settlers

    (1) planted tobacco
    (2) attacked the Native Americans
    (3) searched for gold
    (4) planted food crops
    (5) befriended and helped the Native Americans

17. The colonists needed help from the Native Americans

    (1) because they did not know how to grow tobacco in Virginia
    (2) because they did not produce enough food
    (3) to prevent slavery in Virginia
    (4) to build the village of Jamestown
    (5) to export tobacco to Europe

18. There is enough information in the passage to determine that

   (1) in order to survive, the settlers had to defeat the Native Americans
   (2) the desire for religious freedom was the reason that the settlers came to Virginia
   (3) the settlers needed help from the Native Americans in order to grow tobacco
   (4) the settlers believed in democracy and equality for all people
   (5) the growing and exporting of tobacco led to the success of the Virginia colony

Questions 19–20 are based on the following map.

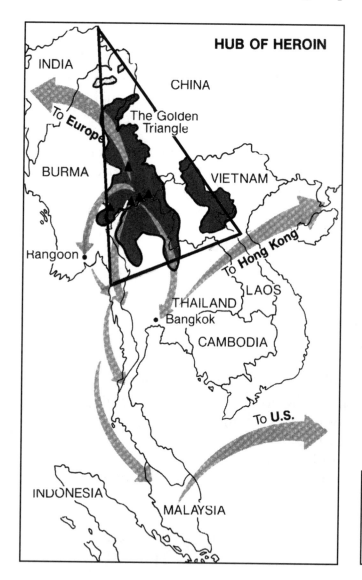

HUB OF HEROIN

INDIA

CHINA

The Golden Triangle

BURMA

VIETNAM

Rangoon

To Europe

To Hong Kong

LAOS

THAILAND
Bangkok

CAMBODIA

To U.S.

INDONESIA

MALAYSIA

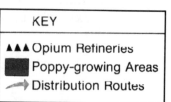

KEY	
▲▲▲	Opium Refineries
■	Poppy-growing Areas
➤	Distribution Routes

19. The opium refineries in the Golden Triangle are all in

    (1) Bangkok
    (2) Europe
    (3) Rangoon
    (4) India
    (5) poppy-growing areas

20. From Malaysia, heroin is sent to

    (1) Thailand
    (2) Burma
    (3) Hong Kong
    (4) the U.S.
    (5) Europe

Questions 21–22 are based on the following passage.

> The plow played a vital role for men in search of the American promise of opportunity and independence. The wilderness was the frontier for American men. As long as they could clear new land, plow it, and grow something on it, it was their land. The plow set them free.
>
> However, the city was the frontier for American women. The typewriter gave them a way to earn money and the opportunity to set a course of their own. The business office, not the wilderness, would give women the chance to control their own lives.

21. According to the passage, the machine that most helped women gain economic independence was

    (1) the sewing machine
    (2) the typewriter
    (3) the plow
    (4) the electric mixer
    (5) the automobile

22. The passage describes different opportunities for American women and American men. The key difference the writer describes is that

    (1) women were more dependent than men
    (2) women preferred to live in cities while men preferred to live in log cabins
    (3) women preferred staying at home while men preferred change and adventure
    (4) cities offered women the independence and opportunity that men found in the wilderness
    (5) women planned for the future while men lived for the present

Questions 23–24 are based on the following passage.

> In the 1840s, many Americans believed in "manifest destiny," the idea that the United States had the right to control all the land from the Atlantic to the Pacific. President Polk used the theory of manifest destiny to justify declaring war on Mexico. As a result of this war, Mexico lost half of its territory and the United States gained most of its southwestern lands, including California.

23. Which of the following statements is an opinion?
    (1) Mexico lost half of its territory after losing the Mexican War.
    (2) The United States took over California as a result of the Mexican War.
    (3) The term *manifest destiny* was coined by John L. O'Sullivan.
    (4) Polk was president of the United States during the Mexican War.
    (5) The United States had the right to take over the entire continent.

24. The main idea of this paragraph is that
    (1) the United States used "manifest destiny" to justify taking over half of Mexico
    (2) Mexico lost half its territory in the Mexican War
    (3) the American form of government needs an entire continent to function well
    (4) the United States was right to conquer half of Mexico in order to spread democracy
    (5) Mexico provoked the United States into war by opposing "manifest destiny"

Question 25 is based on the following advertisement.

> **GIVE HER THE FRAGRANCE OF LUXURY**
> Take her away from the ordinary. Give her something she will never forget. A perfume that says "You're special."
> *Gisell Perfume*
> It costs more, but isn't she worth it?

25. This ad wants you to believe that Gisell perfume
    (1) is used by many famous people
    (2) will make a woman feel special
    (3) is a good buy
    (4) is used by more women than any other perfume
    (5) will drive men wild

Questions 26–28 are based on the following passage.

As in many other southern towns, many people in Eastman, Georgia, used to work in a textile mill. After eighty years of operation, the Reeves Brothers mill closed in the mid '80s, laying off 340 people. The economy of this little town was hurt badly by the loss of jobs and wages from the mill.

Bit by bit, however, the town rebounded from the mill closing. When the mill closed, the Standard Candy Company was run by fewer than 100 part-time employees. Now Standard Candy has several hundred full-time workers. Another company, Reynolds Aluminum, added employees to its payroll. A local welding company expanded, and so did another small candy company. In addition, a large discount store opened its doors in Eastman, providing even more jobs.

Perhaps the biggest boost to Eastman's economy was a new Georgia highway that was built right through it. The highway connects Georgia's largest city, Atlanta, with the Georgia seacoast. Because of the highway, products made in Eastman are easier to ship to other places. The highway also allows Eastman to attract tourists driving from Atlanta to the beaches.

26. The new highway running through Eastman

    (1) runs from Atlanta to New York City
    (2) allows residents to commute easily to work in the textile mill
    (3) attracts tourists driving to Florida
    (4) makes Eastman less attractive to new businesses
    (5) connects Atlanta to the Georgia coast

27. Over the next five years, it is likely that

    (1) more jobs will be created in Eastman
    (2) the population of Eastman will decline rapidly
    (3) many residents of Eastman will turn to farming to make their living
    (4) most people who were laid off when the mill closed will still be out of work
    (5) a major state highway running through Eastman will close

28. Which of the following strategies could best help another small Southern town rebound from a mill closing?

(1) Residents should relocate to areas where mills are still open.
(2) The town should work to attract new businesses to the area.
(3) Mill workers who are laid off by the closing should collect unemployment insurance.
(4) The town should improve schools and recreational programs for children.
(5) The town should build a new highway.

Questions 29–30 are based on the following passage.

Research shows that friendship is very important in the lives of elderly people. A study of senior citizens showed that these older people want to give to and do things for their friends. Researcher Karen Roberto thinks that older people feel more independent and more able when they can give to others.

Roberto also reported that elderly men and elderly women have different kinds of friendships. The men tended to do things with their friends—go places or play games. The women, on the other hand, were more emotionally involved with their friends.

29. According to Roberto, what is a possible reason why elderly people want to give to and do things for their friends?

(1) Many older people don't often see their families, so they want to do things for their friends.
(2) They don't have enough to do to keep busy, and doing things for others helps pass the time.
(3) They feel that their friends are in need of assistance.
(4) Doing things for others makes them feel more independent.
(5) There aren't enough volunteer opportunities for older people.

30. Based on the information in the passage, which of the following statements is true?

(1) Older men are happier with their friendships than older women are.
(2) Elderly people don't have enough friends.
(3) Older men are less emotionally involved with their friends than older women are.
(4) Older people need friends because their families don't care for them.
(5) Senior citizen housing encourages older people to form healthy and lasting friendships.

PRE-TEST EVALUATION CHART

Check your answers on pages 14–15; then come back to this chart and find the number of each question you missed and circle it in the second column. Then decide which chapters you should concentrate on.

	Skill	Question Numbers	Number Correct
Ch. 1	Finding details Words in context Restating information Summarizing information Main idea of a paragraph Main idea of a passage	21, 26 1 2 13 24 3	_____/7
Ch. 2	Locating information on a chart Locating information on a graph Locating information on a map Using a map key	14 11 20 19	_____/4
Ch. 3	Sequence Cause and effect Compare and contrast	8, 16 10 22	_____/4
Ch. 4	Fact and opinion Inference Political cartoons Hypotheses Predicting outcomes	23 17 5, 6, 7 29 27	_____/7
Ch. 5	Adequacy of information Interpreting charts Interpreting graphs Values Propaganda	18, 30 15 12 4 25	_____/6
Ch. 6	Application	9, 28	_____/2

PRE-TEST ANSWER KEY

1. (1) The passage says that 1992 was Sultan Hassanal Bolkiah's 25th year as king. You can conclude that a sultan is a king.

2. (3) The passage tells you that Brunei is ruled by the sultan, who is a king. You can eliminate the other answers.

3. (3) This choice combines all the ideas in the passage: The sultan is very rich; he gives his people a good life, but he controls the government completely.

4. (4) The writer tells you that the companies are most concerned with attendance and punctuality. If a worker comes to work every day on time, the worker is dependable.

5. (1) The speaker is holding a gavel and assigning punishment.

6. (4) Some game shows, like "The Price Is Right," offer contestants mystery boxes like the one in this cartoon.

7. (1) The gift-wrapped door represents the alternative sentence. If the defendant is lucky, the sentence will be light; if he's unlucky, the sentence will be heavy.

8. (1) The passage states that, after she signed the sales slip, Caroline left the store.

9. (3) A shoe store is the only place among the choices where you could buy something in person with a credit card.

10. (3) The passage says that Caroline could not afford to pay the whole amount she owed. As a result, she had to pay interest on the remaining amount.

11. (2) The highest point on the graph is labeled 1965.

12. (1) In 1965, there was an average of 2.44 children per household. In 1985, that number had dropped to 1.85. With fewer children per household, you could conclude that children have fewer brothers and sisters.

13. (1) The passage describes different ways that the United States has been a world leader in transportation.

14. (3) Find the column labeled "Chromium." Then find the row labeled "Share of U.S. imports originating in South Africa." The percentage in the box where the row and column cross is 43%.

15. (4) These materials are important to U.S. industry. The chart shows you that South Africa sells a lot of these materials to the United States.

16. (3) The passage states that the colonists built their village and then spent their time looking for gold.

17. (2) The passage tells you that the entire colony would have starved if Powhatan had not given the settlers food. A likely explanation for this situation is that the settlers were not producing enough food.

18. (5) The passage states that the colony limped along until Rolfe discovered tobacco and that Virginia began exporting tobacco to Europe. The writer concludes by saying that the success of the Virginia colony was assured, implying that tobacco was the reason for that success.

19. (5) Opium refineries are marked on the map by triangles. All the triangles are in the poppy-growing areas (shaded gray).

20. (4) Distribution routes are marked on the map by arrows. The arrow from Malaysia, in the bottom center of the map, is labeled "to U.S."

21. (2) The passage says that the typewriter gave women a way to earn money.

22. (4) The first paragraph says that men found independence in the wilderness. The second paragraph describes the city as the place where women found the opportunity for independence.

23. (5) Many Americans believed this idea, but it was their opinion, not a fact. All the other choices are facts.

24. (1) This choice pulls together all the ideas in the paragraph.

25. (2) The ad tells you that giving a woman the perfume says to her, "You're special."

26. (5) The passage says that the highway connects Atlanta with the Georgia seacoast.

27. (1) The passage describes ways in which new jobs are coming into Eastman because of new and expanding businesses. It also states that the highway helps Eastman's manufacturing and tourist businesses.

28. (2) New businesses are helping to bring new jobs to Eastman. Other small towns that have lost jobs through mill closings would also benefit if new businesses moved in.

29. (4) The passage tells you that Roberto thinks that older people feel more independent when they can give to others.

30. (3) The passage tells you that men tended to do things with their friends while women were more emotionally involved with their friends.

CHAPTER 1

UNDERSTANDING WHAT YOU READ

In order to understand social studies fully, you will need to master the skills in this book. One of the most basic reading skills is finding details and facts. Another basic reading skill is understanding the meaning of unfamiliar words. In this chapter, you'll work on these two skills.

Later in the chapter, you'll work on putting ideas in other words by summarizing and restating. Then you'll practice finding the main idea. Studying these skills will lay the groundwork for reading and understanding social studies.

LOCATING DETAILS AND FACTS

QUESTION WORDS

The first step in understanding what you read is picking out **details**. You look for facts to answer six basic questions: Who? What? Where? When? How? and Why? In the following example, Judge Phillips needs to use all six questions in order to understand the case.

> **JUDGE:** *Whom* are you here to represent?
>
> **LAWYER:** My client is Elisa Canter.
>
> **JUDGE:** *Why* is she here?

LAWYER: To sue the McWatt Shoe Company.

JUDGE: *What* are the grounds for the suit?

LAWYER: Manufacturing a faulty pair of boots that caused an injury.

JUDGE: *When* did this alleged injury take place?

LAWYER: Last Friday night.

JUDGE: *Where* did it happen?

LAWYER: At Ms. Canter's home.

JUDGE: *How* did the boots cause the injury?

LAWYER: The soles stuck to a patch of ice, causing her to fall.

In order for the judge to make a decision, she must ask *who, what, when, where, how,* and *why.* To understand the details of what you read, you should be able to find the answers to these questions.

FINDING THE INFORMATION

Now practice finding information for questions asking *who, what, when, where, how,* and *why.* Read the following paragraph in which the speaker describes his memories of a bread line. See if you can match the correct answer with each question. Write the letter of the answer in the space provided.

> I was walking along the street at that time (1932), and you'd see the bread lines. The biggest one in New York City was owned by William Randolph Hearst. He had a big truck with several people on it, and big cauldrons of hot soup, bread. Fellows with burlap on their feet were lined up all around Columbus Circle, and went for blocks and blocks around the park, waiting.

_____ 1. Where was this bread line?

(a) He had a big truck with several people on it.

_____ 2. Who was waiting in the bread line?

(b) in 1932

(c) in New York City

_____ 3. When did this scene take place?

(d) fellows with burlap on their feet

_____ 4. What was being served at the bread line?

(e) hot soup and bread

_____ 5. How did William Randolph Hearst give out food to poor people?

Make sure you tried each question in the example above on your own before you read the following explanations. Did you match one answer to each question?

1. (c) To answer this *where* question, you must find the name of the place. The place is given in the second sentence: New York City.

2. (d) To answer this *who* question, you must find the name or a description of people in the bread line. They are described in the last sentence: "Fellows with burlap on their feet were lined up. . . ."

3. (b) To answer this *when* question, you must find the date. In the first sentence, 1932 is given as the year the events of the passage took place.

4. (e) To answer this *what* question, you must look for the name or description of the thing served. In the third sentence, you read that hot soup and bread were served on the truck.

5. (a) To answer this *how* question, you must find the way Hearst gave out the food. The third sentence states, "He had a big truck with several people on it. . . ."

EXERCISE 1: FINDING DETAILS

Directions: Following each paragraph are detail questions. Write your answer to each question in the space provided.

> In 1960, television helped elect a new president. Young John Kennedy defeated Richard Nixon in their famous television debates. Many political writers believe that Kennedy's good performance on television led to his narrow victory in the election.

1. Who were involved in the important televised debates of 1960?

   _____

2. According to many political writers, how did Kennedy win the 1960 presidential election?

   _____

In 1968, the Public Service Company of New Hampshire began building a nuclear power plant in Seabrook, New Hampshire. It took twenty years to open the plant, and the Public Service Company went bankrupt in the process. There were construction delays and funding problems, but the biggest headache was protesters. They occupied the plant site and the governor's office. They disrupted public hearings and interfered with plant procedures. Eventually, their fight became a symbol of success for anti-nuclear protesters across the nation. Nevertheless, the Seabrook plant opened in 1990. The controversy, however, continues. Now, the Nuclear Regulatory Commission (NRC) is under fire for lying to Congress about safety inspections at the plant.

3. Where is the power plant located?

    _____

4. When did the plant open?

    _____

5. How did protesters let the governor of New Hampshire know about their concerns?

    _____

6. Why is the plant controversial today?

    _____

Answers start on page 198.

EXERCISE 2: MORE PRACTICE IN FINDING DETAILS

Directions: This exercise is in multiple-choice format. Read the paragraphs. Then answer the questions that follow.

When George L. Belair was running for city council in Minneapolis, Minnesota, he gave away some Twinkies to senior citizens. Under Minnesota law, candidates for office are not allowed to give away food or drinks in order to get votes. Because of this law, Mr. Belair was arrested. He had to prove in court that he was not trying to get votes by giving away the cakes.

1. To whom did Mr. Belair give the Twinkies?

    (1) the court
    (2) his opponent
    (3) the city council
    (4) senior citizens
    (5) candidates

2. Why was Mr. Belair arrested?

(1) He tried to bribe a police officer by giving him Twinkies.
(2) It's illegal to give away a product that people usually have to pay for.
(3) He had stolen the Twinkies he was giving away.
(4) He gave free drinks to senior citizens.
(5) In Minnesota, candidates cannot give away food to get votes.

Since 1945, the human race has had to face the possibility of its own destruction. In August of that year, an American airplane dropped the first atomic bomb on Hiroshima, Japan. That single bomb destroyed the entire city. In the years since that first explosion, the United States has built enough bombs to destroy the entire world. The Soviet Union has also built enough bombs to wipe out the human race. Great Britain, France, India, and China also have nuclear weapons. Humanity's future now depends on countries settling their differences peacefully.

3. The first atomic bomb was dropped by

(1) the Soviet Union
(2) the United States
(3) Germany
(4) Japan
(5) China

4. What was the result when the bomb was dropped on Hiroshima?

(1) The United Nations was formed.
(2) The Soviet Union built many bombs.
(3) The entire city was destroyed.
(4) The United States destroyed the entire world.
(5) An American airplane went down.

For many years, large companies have fought with their workers' unions. But greater competition from overseas has forced both sides to look again at the way they work together. One example of a new approach occurred at the Chrysler Corporation. The United Auto Workers worked together with the company and the government to save Chrysler. Workers accepted pay cuts while the company got back on its feet. The president of the auto workers' union became a member of the board of directors. During the crisis, workers and management tried to become partners instead of enemies.

5. Why did the union and Chrysler management decide to work together?

    (1) The government forced them to work together.
    (2) The union president joined the board of directors.
    (3) The company got tired of fighting with the union.
    (4) Greater competition from overseas threatened the company.
    (5) Workers and management wanted to become partners.

6. Who accepted pay cuts while Chrysler got back on its feet?

    (1) large companies
    (2) the union president
    (3) the board of directors
    (4) management
    (5) workers

Answers start on page 198.

UNDERSTANDING UNFAMILIAR WORDS

USING THE CONTEXT

When reading social studies, you may find unfamiliar words. When you see words you don't know, understanding what you read is harder. Until you figure out the unknown word, what you read might not make sense to you.

You could find out the meaning of a word by looking it up in the dictionary. But sometimes you can't do that—you don't have time, or no dictionary is handy. And even if you do look up a word in the dictionary, sometimes the definition is hard to understand. However, you can often figure out the meaning of a word by reading the words around it. This is called using the *context* (words around a word) to figure out the meaning of an unknown word. In this section, you'll practice looking at the context of unfamiliar words to find their meanings.

SYNONYM, DEFINITION, AND COMPARISON CLUES

Often in social studies reading, you will find a *synonym*—another word with almost the same meaning—near an unfamiliar word. Or you might find an explanation or definition of what the unknown word means. Sometimes in the passage you will find a comparison with something you know or understand. All of these clues can help you figure out what the unknown word means. Here's an example:

> Calvin Coolidge once said, "When more and more people are thrown out of work, **unemployment** results."

In this example, there is a definition clue. The word *unemployment* is explained directly in the sentence. Underline the definition of *unemployment* in the quotation above. Unemployment happens when people are thrown out of work.

Now try another example. Underline the comparison in the following passage that is a clue to the meaning of the word *homogeneous*.

> The girls at Whitman High School can only be described as **homogeneous**. Like a school of identically shaped and colored fish, they wear the same clothes, eat the same food, and even talk the same.

▶ What does *homogeneous* mean? _____

Homogeneous means "alike." The comparison clue is "Like a school of identically shaped and colored fish . . . ." In addition, the passage says that the girls dress, eat, and talk alike.

EXERCISE 3: SYNONYM, DEFINITION, AND COMPARISON CLUES

Directions: In the space provided, write the meaning of the word or phrase in **dark type**. Use the context clues in the sentences—look for a synonym, definition, or comparison.

1. The **Bessemer process** of steel making consists of blowing air through molten iron to get rid of impurities.

   Bessemer process _____

2. Like the patent medicine sold by phony doctors to cure all kinds of illnesses, industrial growth was supposed to be a **panacea** for the nation's ills.

   panacea _____

3. President Andrew Jackson began a dubious American political tradition, the widespread use of **patronage**—giving jobs and favors for political reasons.

   patronage _____

4. De Beers Company created a **monopoly** in the diamond industry, controlling production and crushing its competition.

   monopoly _____

5. Worker **productivity** has increased as new machines allow one laborer to make much more than before.

    productivity _____

6. When the **transcontinental** railroad was completed in 1869, a person could travel by train from the Atlantic to the Pacific Ocean.

    transcontinental _____

Answers start on page 198.

ANTONYM AND CONTRAST CLUES

In the last section you learned how to figure out the meaning of a word when nearby words had a similar meaning. In this section, you will figure out the meaning of an unknown word when the nearby words have an *opposite* meaning. Read the example sentence below.

> As the strike entered its ninth week, the workers had to decide whether to **persist** or to give up.

▶ What does *persist* mean? _____

This example has an antonym clue. An **antonym** is a word that is the opposite of a given word. In this example, the workers are choosing between two choices: to persist or *to give up*. You can conclude that the opposite of *to persist* is *to give up*. Therefore, *to persist* means *to keep trying*. Now try another example.

> Despite government claims that people were calming down, the violence continued to **escalate**.

▶ What is the meaning of *escalate*? _____

This example has a contrast clue. A situation is described that is **in contrast to**, or the opposite of, another situation. In this sentence, *escalating violence* is the opposite of people becoming calm. You can conclude that **to escalate** means *to increase*.

Clue words such as *unlike*, *despite*, and *although* may help you identify antonym and contrast clues, as in the following example:

> **Unlike** children in **wealthy** Kenwood, many children in **impoverished** Garfield Park go hungry.

EXERCISE 4: ANTONYM AND CONTRAST CLUES

Directions: The sentences on the left have antonym or contrast clues. Each sentence contains words or phrases with opposite meanings. Choose the letter of the correct answer to each question on the right.

After years without restrictions on the number of immigrants allowed into the country, Congress passed the first **quota** law in 1921.

1. A quota is
    (a) a person from another country
    (b) a numerical limit
    (c) an economic goal

In the late nineteenth century, new cities grew in the Northeast and Midwest. The **squalor** of these new industrial cities contrasted sharply with the beauty of the surrounding countryside.

2. Squalor is
    (a) filth
    (b) large size
    (c) beauty

After living in the well-watered East, many pioneers were unprepared for the **arid** West.

3. According to the passage, the West was
    (a) well-watered
    (b) dry
    (c) empty

Despite the desire of Native Americans to live **amicably** with white people, treaties were broken and fighting broke out.

4. To live amicably is to
    (a) control others
    (b) be peaceful
    (c) better oneself

Unlike the Native American tribes, who only wanted to keep their own lands, the United States followed an **expansionist** policy in the nineteenth century.

5. An expansionist policy favors
    (a) improving relations with neighbors
    (b) getting rid of foreign influence
    (c) making the nation larger

Answers start on page 198.

USING THE SENSE OF THE PASSAGE

Sometimes an important word is not defined directly. There may not be any antonyms or contrast clues. In these cases, you must determine the meaning of the word by reading the entire passage. Sometimes you might be able to figure out the meaning of the unknown word by looking at examples given in the rest of the passage. Other times you will have to rely on your overall understanding of the meaning of the passage, as in the following example.

> The great American **megalopolis** stretches over four hundred miles from Boston to Washington, D.C. Including such cities as New York, Newark, Philadelphia, and Baltimore, it is the largest urban area in the United States.

▶ What is a megalopolis?

    (1) a large city and its suburbs
    (2) a state government
    (3) a group of connected cities and suburbs
    (4) a large lottery

You were right if you chose (3). The phrase *stretches over* gives you the sense of a connected or continuous area. Since the megalopolis includes many cities, it would have to include suburban areas lying between the cities.

EXERCISE 5: USING THE SENSE OF THE PASSAGE

Directions: Answer the questions that follow each passage.

> At **the turn of the century**, American life was changing rapidly. The most visible change was in transportation. Cars were beginning to be seen all over the country. And in 1903, the Wright brothers made the first airplane flight. Motorized vehicles were becoming our primary way of getting around.

1. When is meant by *the turn of the century* in this passage?
    (1) around 1700
    (2) around 1800
    (3) around 1900
    (4) in 1903

> **Congestion** in a big city can't be avoided. One experiences it everywhere. Traffic jams are a constant irritation, making one's feet the fastest way to travel most of the time. A crowded elevator and a tightly packed subway train are other reminders of congestion in the city. One can't even escape from lack of space by dying, since cemeteries are just as densely populated as the cities they serve.

2. *Congestion* means

   (1) illness
   (2) confusion
   (3) overcrowding
   (4) poverty

> She was a scrawny hardbitten little woman and she greeted me with that politely blank stare which Negroes often reserve for hostile whites or prying members of their own race.
>
> I had been directed to her tenement in Richmond's **ramshackle** Negro section by another woman, a gray-haired old grandmother whose **gnarled** hands had been stemming tobacco for five decades.

3. *Ramshackle* means

   (1) run-down
   (2) modern
   (3) quaint
   (4) historic

4. *Gnarled* means

   (1) pretty
   (2) smooth
   (3) twisted
   (4) black

Answers start on page 198.

RESTATING AND SUMMARIZING

RESTATING DETAILS AND FACTS

> "Mom, you're going to love your new home. There will be people there your own age. There will be a nurse on duty at all times. You'll get the medical care you need."
>
> "So you've decided to ship your poor old mother to a nursing home."

Mom has just restated the facts in different words. Being able to *restate* details and facts in different words is an important step in understanding what you read. Here's an example of a passage and questions that ask you to identify material that is stated in different words.

(1) One way out pointed north. (2) There were jobs up there, people said. (3) And they let you live a little. (4) The war that had exploded in Europe in 1914 had cut off the flow of immigrants from the old countries. (5) Northern factories, booming on war orders, were short of labor. (6) Manufacturers sent agents south to recruit black workers. (7) They came with free railroad passes in hand or offered cheap tickets to groups of migrants. (8) A "Northern fever" seized the Blacks of the South.

Read the following statements. If the statement is a correct restatement of the sentence or sentences indicated, write *C* in the blank and underline the part of the passage it restates. If not, write *I* for incorrect.

_____ 1. Northern manufacturers preferred southern black workers to European immigrants. (sentences *4–5*)

_____ 2. Employers gave southern blacks assistance in moving north to work. (sentence *7*)

Read the following explanations to see how you could think through this example correctly:

1. I   The passage states that the war in Europe had cut off the flow of immigrants and the factories were short of labor. It doesn't say anything about what kind of workers the manufacturers preferred.

2. C   This sentence restates the information in sentence *7*. The passage says that the agents of manufacturers encouraged blacks to go north to work by giving them free or cheap railroad tickets.

EXERCISE 6: RECOGNIZING RESTATED INFORMATION

Directions: After reading each passage, read the sentences that follow. If you think that the statement is a correct restatement of part of the passage, write *C* for correct. If not, write *I* for incorrect.

(1) We had good schools in French Corral, better than they had in San Francisco at that time. (2) Most of our teachers were young men who were college graduates out from the East for a chance to make money and go back to take up further studies. (3) One of our best teachers was Marion McCarroll Scott, a young Southerner. (4) The various teachers found a congenial atmosphere in our home and spent many evenings playing cards with my parents.

_____ 1. The young teachers who came to French Corral from the East wanted to start a new life and settle there. (sentence *2*)

_____ **2.** Teachers were always welcome in the writer's home. (sentence *4*)

(1) For many years, the United States has interfered in the affairs of Nicaragua. (2) In the 1850s, Cornelius Vanderbilt organized a steamboat company to transport freight across Nicaragua. (3) Because Vanderbilt wanted political stability in the region, he financed William Walker to overthrow the existing government. (4) In 1856, Walker became president of Nicaragua.

(5) Walker made the mistake of quarreling with Vanderbilt and seizing his ships. (6) This led to an invasion of Nicaragua by a Central American coalition supported by Vanderbilt. (7) This coalition deposed President William Walker.

_____ **3.** Vanderbilt worked for the establishment of democracy in Nicaragua. (sentence *3*)

_____ **4.** Walker lost his presidency when he lost Vanderbilt's support. (sentences *6–7*)

Answers start on page 198.

EXERCISE 7: RESTATING INFORMATION IN YOUR OWN WORDS

Directions: Read each passage. Then, in your own words, answer the questions that follow.

Rockefeller's company, Standard Oil, managed to put a lot of other oil companies out of business. First Rockefeller pressured railroads into lowering their freight charges for Standard Oil shipments. Then he could charge less for his products than other oil companies because his freight costs were lower. If other oil companies managed to stay in business anyway, Rockefeller had another tactic. He would lower his prices in their area until Standard Oil had lured away all the other companies' customers.

1. How did Standard Oil reduce its freight costs?

_____

2. How did Standard Oil wipe out its competition?

_____

The most successful of the early labor unions was the American Federation of Labor (AFL), founded in 1886 under the leadership of Samuel Gompers. The AFL was a united group of craft unions. Unlike the unsuccessful labor unions, the AFL did not sponsor its own political candidates. It also did not demand radical social change. Instead, the AFL worked toward concrete goals such as higher wages and shorter work hours.

3. What kinds of goals did the American Federation of Labor work toward?

_____

4. What did the unsuccessful early labor unions do?

_____

Answers start on page 199.

SUMMARIZING DETAILS AND FACTS

When you summarize, you make one statement that gives the main point of a group of details or facts. A summary should contain all of the important ideas. In the following example, practice finding a summary statement that pulls together all the ideas in the original sentences. Read the following three statements:

Henry Ford produced the first low-cost automobile.

Ford was able to save money through mass production of his automobile.

Millions of people were able to own a car for the first time because of the low cost.

Now place a check before the sentence that best summarizes the three statements. Make sure the one you choose contains all of the important ideas from the three statements.

_____ Mass production has made many products affordable.
_____ By creating the mass-produced car, Henry Ford changed America.
_____ By using mass production, Ford produced a low-cost car that was bought by millions of people.

The last choice is the correct one: By using mass production (second statement), Ford produced a low-cost car (first statement) that was bought by millions of people (third statement). You can see that all the important ideas are covered.

EXERCISE 8: SUMMARIZING FACTS

Directions: Following each group of statements are three possible summary sentences. Circle the letter of the best summary. Make sure all the important ideas are included in the summary you choose.

1. Coleco almost went bankrupt trying to sell video game machines.
   The Cabbage Patch doll was a huge success.
   Coleco markets the Cabbage Patch doll.

   (a) The Cabbage Patch doll was a successful product for Coleco.
   (b) After failing with video game machines, Coleco was saved by the Cabbage Patch doll.
   (c) Coleco was unable to sell video game machines successfully.

2. AT&T's monopoly of long-distance service has ended.
   MCI and Sprint now offer long-distance telephone service.
   AT&T has had to lay off workers in order to remain competitive.

   (a) MCI and Sprint are the telephone companies of the future.
   (b) The ending of the AT&T telephone monopoly has led to competition and worker layoffs.
   (c) The AT&T telephone monopoly was in violation of anti-trust laws.

3. Hospital costs are higher than most people can afford.
   An unexpected illness can be a financial disaster for a family.
   Medical insurance pays for hospital costs and doctors' bills.

   (a) Medical insurance protects people from large health-care bills.
   (b) The United States should adopt a National Health Insurance plan.
   (c) Medical costs are too high and should be reduced to help protect families.

Answers start on page 199.

PUTTING THE DETAILS TOGETHER

TOPIC AND MAIN IDEA

You have practiced finding, understanding, restating, and summarizing details so far in this chapter. The next step is to start putting these details together. To get a complete picture of what the writer is talking about, you must determine the topic and the main idea.

The *topic* is the subject of a passage. The **main idea** is the point the writer wants to make about the topic. The details provide evidence or examples or description to explain the main idea to you.

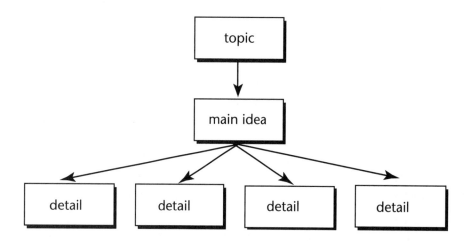

IDENTIFYING THE TOPIC

In the last exercise of the previous section, you summarized details and facts from three statements. You're now going to work with paragraphs. A *paragraph* is a group of sentences that help develop a central point or idea.

The topic is what the paragraph is about. One way to determine the topic of a paragraph is to look at the details. Study the details in the paragraph below. Do they suggest a topic, a subject that the whole paragraph relates to?

> The Federal Reserve controls the nation's money supply. Most people need to budget their money very carefully. Many products cater to young consumers. It is very hard to survive on welfare.

You probably are not sure what the topic of this group of sentences is. In fact, there is no single topic. These sentences look like a paragraph, but they are not. For a group of sentences to be a paragraph, they must be about a single topic.

The example that follows is a unified paragraph except for one thing: it contains a sentence that does not belong. Read the paragraph carefully. Decide what the topic of the paragraph is. Then identify the sentence that is not about the topic.

> (1) Today many people do much of their banking by automatic teller machine (ATM). (2) These ATMs can be found in many places, including department stores and supermarkets. (3) Banks supply their customers with access cards for the machines. (4) You can pay for groceries by check at many supermarkets. (5) Most automatic teller machines can give you money from your account, tell you your account balance, or let you make a deposit.

▶ What is the topic of this paragraph? _____

▶ Which sentence does not belong? _____

The topic of this paragraph is *automatic teller machines*. Each sentence is related to this topic except for sentence *4*. Sentence *4* is about money, but it is not about automatic teller machines.

EXERCISE 9: IDENTIFYING UNRELATED SENTENCES

Directions: In each of the following paragraphs, one sentence does not belong. Read each paragraph carefully to find its topic. Then fill in the blank with the letter of the sentence that does not belong.

_____ 1. (a) Tanya bought a brand-new car. (b) Within six months the car had broken down eight times. (c) Under her state's "lemon" law, the car dealer had to replace the defective car. (d) Used car prices have gone up in recent years.

_____ 2. (a) Japanese products are very popular with American consumers. (b) For many years now, Americans have been buying a wide variety of these products, including cars, stereos, and VCRs. (c) The American automobile industry is making a comeback. (d) Japanese restaurants are now becoming very popular in the United States. (e) Sushi, a Japanese dish, is almost as well known to Americans as products made by Sony, a Japanese manufacturer.

_____ 3. (a) The Consumer Price Index (CPI) measures the inflation rate. (b) The cost of housing is a major factor in the CPI. (c) Food prices often depend on the weather. (d) Food and clothing costs are also major factors in the CPI. (e) As housing, food, and clothing costs rise, so does the Consumer Price Index.

_____ 4. (a) One hundred years ago, most textiles used by Americans were made in the northeastern United States. (b) Then, looking for cheaper labor, many manufacturers moved to the southeastern United States. (c) In recent years, textile manufacturing has moved again. (d) Now the cheap labor is in eastern Asia, so most textiles are now made there. (e) Korea, Japan, Taiwan, and Hong Kong are all major trading partners with our country.

Answers start on page 199.

FINDING THE MAIN IDEA

Every paragraph has a topic, the subject of the paragraph. And every paragraph has a main idea. The *main idea* is the most important thing, or the central point, that the writer wants to say about the topic. Practice finding the topic and the main idea in the following example paragraph. Read the paragraph; then answer the questions that follow it.

> In our free enterprise system, anyone has the right to go into business. If you see a need, you do not have to have government permission to try to fill it. Whether it is a new computer company or a roadside fruit stand, you have the right to try to sell your products. And if you are successful, the rewards can be great.

▶ What is the topic of this paragraph? _____
▶ What do you think the writer's main point is? _____
   _____

You were right if you said that the topic is "starting a business in our free enterprise system." Each sentence is related to this topic. The main idea is more specific than the topic. The main idea is stated in the first sentence, "In our free enterprise system, anyone has the right to go into business." This main idea tells you the central point of the rest of the sentences. You'll get more practice identifying the main idea on the following pages.

Now try another example. After the following paragraph are four choices for main idea. Circle the letter of the best choice for the main idea.

> In past decades, most developing countries borrowed billions of dollars from large banks. Today, those loans threaten the world economy. Many developing countries, like Argentina and Brazil, have trouble repaying their loans. Since the world banking system would collapse if the loans went bad, the banks lend these nations more money to pay off their debts. Because of this cycle of borrowing, the world faces a debt crisis.

▶ What is the main idea of this paragraph?

(a) Argentina is having trouble paying back its debts.
(b) The world economy is threatened by a debt crisis.
(c) Today, the world economy has made all countries interdependent.
(d) The United States economy is the largest in the world.

You were correct if you chose (b). It sums up the central point of the paragraph. Choice (a) is too narrow because it is only a specific detail mentioned in the paragraph. Choice (c) is too broad and general. The main idea of this paragraph is more specific—*debt* in the world economy. Choice (d) is not mentioned in the passage at all.

EXERCISE 10: IDENTIFYING THE MAIN IDEA

Directions: Following each paragraph are four choices for main idea. Put *M* by the main idea. Put *N* by the choice that is too narrow. Put *B* by the choice that is too broad. Put *X* by the choice that is not in the passage.

1. Children are a major target of television advertising. Some consumer groups are concerned about the results of targeting these young viewers. Exciting ads and magical promises can easily convince children that they must have the newest toy. Children then pressure their parents to buy toys that the family may not be able to afford. This problem can lead to overspending by the parents or very disappointed children.

_____ (a) Television ads are usually aimed at a specific target group.
_____ (b) Children are easily convinced by exciting TV ads that they must have the newest toy.
_____ (c) Magazine ads aimed at teenagers could disrupt families.
_____ (d) Consumer groups are concerned about the results of TV ads for children.

2. In a capitalist economy, most factories and farms are privately owned. In a socialist economy, the society as a whole owns the factories and the farms. Until recently, the Chinese had a socialist economy. But in recent years, the Chinese government has begun to experiment with private ownership. The Chinese are trying to combine the best of socialism and capitalism. In time, perhaps they will develop a completely new kind of economy.

_____ (a) Capitalism and socialism are the two main economic systems in the world.
_____ (b) China is experimenting with combining capitalism with socialism
_____ (c) China has successfully controlled the growth of its population.
_____ (d) Most factories and farms are privately owned in a capitalist economy.

3. One measure of a healthy economy is the savings rate. The savings rate measures how much money people deposit in savings accounts. A savings account is a cushion against hard times. It is also a source of money for investment. In the United States, the savings rate is very low. Because of the low savings rate, the United States economy has less money available for investment and less protection against hard times than a country with a higher savings rate has.

_____ (a) The low savings rate in the United States weakens the economy.
_____ (b) A savings account is a cushion against hard times.
_____ (c) The United States faces economic hard times.
_____ (d) Saving rates are important.

Answers start on page 199.

TOPIC SENTENCES

As you have already seen, the main idea of a paragraph is sometimes stated directly in one of the sentences of the paragraph. This sentence is called the *topic sentence*. The topic sentence is often at the beginning of a paragraph. The topic sentence may also occur at the end or sometimes even in the middle of a paragraph. No matter where the topic sentence appears in the paragraph, all other sentences relate to it. They are *supporting* sentences—they support the main idea expressed in the topic sentence.

See if you can find the topic sentence in the following paragraph. If you can find the topic sentence, underline it.

The Environmental Protection Agency (EPA) is responsible for the quality of our environment. The EPA enforces the Clean Water and Clean Air Acts. It must protect wetlands and other delicate ecosystems. In addition, toxic wastes and their disposal are the EPA's responsibility.

You were right if you underlined the first sentence. It introduces the main idea of the paragraph, that the EPA is responsible for the quality of the environment. The other three sentences all give examples of the EPA's responsibilities.

In the following example paragraph, the topic sentence has been replaced by a blank line. Read the paragraph carefully and answer the two questions below.

▶ What is the topic? _____

▶ What is the main point being made about the topic? _____

_____

Now write a topic sentence for the paragraph that expresses the main idea.

_____

_____ Only about half of all employees in the United States work a "standard" work week of thirty-five to forty-five hours. Almost a quarter of all employees work fewer than thirty-five hours. The rest work more than forty-five hours each week. However, experts think that these statistics don't tell the whole story. In reality, many of those thirty-five- to forty-five-hour workers may actually work much longer hours.

You were right if you said the topic of the paragraph is the number of hours people work each week. The writer's main point is that the forty-hour work week is probably not usual for U.S. workers. A good topic sentence for the paragraph might be something like this: *A forty-hour work week is probably not standard for most workers in the United States.*

EXERCISE 11: WRITING TOPIC SENTENCES

Directions: In each of the following paragraphs, the topic sentence has been replaced by a blank line. Read the paragraph and answer the questions. Then, on the first line of the paragraph, write a topic sentence that introduces the main idea of the paragraph.

1. What is the topic? _____

   What is the main point being made about the topic?

   _____

   _____

   _____ The Federal Deposit Insurance Corporation (FDIC) was established in the 1930s after many people lost their life savings when banks failed. Today most bank accounts are insured by the FDIC up to a fixed amount. As a result, if a bank fails, the FDIC will replace money that depositors had in accounts at the failed bank.

2. What is the topic? _____

What is the main point being made about the topic?

_____

_____

_____ One common kind of consumer co-op is housing co-ops. Housing co-ops are owned jointly by the members who live in them. Another common type of consumer co-op is food co-ops. Food co-ops can be large supermarkets or small health-food stores. These co-ops are owned by the members who shop there. Child-care co-ops are preschools and day-care centers owned by members, the parents of the children who attend them.

3. What is the topic? _____ _____

What is the main point being made about the topic?

_____

_____

_____ One of the problems Shirley had to face was how to pay for her increasing heating bills on her senior citizen's fixed income. She faced a similar problem with her phone bill. And finally she had to deal with the problem of rising property taxes. She was afraid that she would have to sell the house she had lived in for forty-five years.

Answers start on page 199.

FINDING THE MAIN IDEA OF A PASSAGE

The same process used in finding the main idea of a paragraph is used in finding the main idea of a passage. If you find the main idea of each paragraph in a passage, you will find that they are related. They all point to one overriding main idea for the passage as a whole. Read the following newspaper article about the 1996 primary elections in New Hampshire. What is the main idea of the first paragraph? the second? the third? What is the one main idea that sums up the whole passage?

Before every presidential election, the Democratic and Republican parties conduct statewide primary elections to measure the popularity of candidates. The nation's first primary election, in New Hampshire, is a presidential candidate's first and probably most powerful opportunity to impress party officials and capture public attention. Successful candidates in the New Hampshire primary usually do well nationwide.

Although the upcoming New Hampshire primary is months away, possible Republican presidential candidates seem to be making appearances everywhere. The Republican frontrunner,

Senator Bob Dole, is planning a 10-day campaign tour of New Hampshire. Former Tennessee governor Lamar Alexander ishiking border-to-border across the state. Bob Dole, Phil Gramm, Pete Wilson, and Lamar Alexander were all here last week.

But presidential campaigns involve more than speeches. The Republican candidates will try various strategies in New Hampshire. Governor Alexander began airing campaign commercials months ago.   Before dropping out of the race, California governor Pete Wilson pointedly selected a popular New England politician as his new national finance chairman. Wilson's campaign strategists had hoped the chairman's New Hampshire supporters would follow him into Wilson's camp. Dole's staff has already completed direct-mail campaigns and telephone surveys. Like other presidential candidates, Senator Dole is also softening his most liberal positions to reassure conservative New Hampshire voters.

main idea of first paragraph: _____

_____

main idea of second paragraph: _____

_____

main idea of third paragraph: _____

_____

Did you fill in an answer close to the following ones for the main idea of each paragraph? The main idea of the first paragraph is that doing well in the New Hampshire primary is very important to presidential candidates. The main idea of the second paragraph is that candidates are starting to make campaign visits to the state. The main idea of the third paragraph is that the candidates will try many strategies in their New Hampshire campaigns.

Now you have looked at the main idea of each paragraph separately. But what about the passage as a whole? What is the main point the writer is trying to make? Look again at the main ideas for each of the three paragraphs. The main idea of the passage summarizes the main ideas of the individual paragraphs.

Write a main idea for the passage: _____

_____

_____

You might have written something like this:

> Winning the New Hampshire primary is very important to presidential candidates, so they will be trying many strategies to win votes there.

Did the main idea you wrote contain all the important points?

EXERCISE 12: MAIN IDEA OF A PASSAGE

Directions: Read the following passage. Then choose the correct main idea for each of the three paragraphs. Finally, choose the main idea for the passage.

(1) The Chicago Housing Authority (CHA) has decided to allow renters in one city housing project to manage the project themselves. The tenants of the LeClaire Courts complex have worked toward this decision for three years. They say that tenant management has made living conditions better in housing projects in other large cities.

(2) The new tenant managers will have almost complete control of their housing complex. They will take care of their own maintenance and security and select new tenants. In addition, the CHA has set aside $1 million for repairs in the complex. Residents will decide how the money will be spent. However, the tenant managers will report to the CHA's board of directors.

(3) LeClaire tenants have already formed a management company. A group of about fifteen tenants will be given an intensive three-month training program to learn to manage the housing project. Then they may have as much as two years' follow-up training. When their training period is over, the CHA will allow the tenant company to take over the complex.

1. The main idea of paragraph *1* is

    (a) the CHA is going to allow tenants of a housing project to manage it themselves
    (b) tenant management lowers the quality of life in housing projects
    (c) tenant management has succeeded in other major cities
    (d) LeClaire tenants have worked toward tenant management for three years

2. The main idea of paragraph *2* is

    (a) the CHA has set aside $1 million to repair the housing project
    (b) the CHA will decide how to use the repair money set aside for LeClaire Courts
    (c) the tenant managers will have almost complete control over LeClaire Courts
    (d) the tenant managers will have to report to the CHA's board of directors

3. The main idea of paragraph *3* is

   (a) the LeClaire tenants have formed a tenant management company
   (b) about 15 tenants will actually manage the complex
   (c) after tenant managers are trained, the tenant company will run the complex
   (d) the tenant managers will not need special training to manage the complex

4. Choose the sentence below that best summarizes the main idea of the entire passage you have just read. Use the main ideas of the individual paragraphs to help you choose the main idea of the passage.

   (a) Tenants lost their battle for control of the LeClaire Courts CHA housing project.
   (b) Following a training period, the CHA board will give a group of tenants almost complete control of their housing project.
   (c) Tenants will be deciding how to spend $1 million in rehab money at the CHA's LeClaire Courts development.
   (d) Tenant management has improved living conditions in public housing in several major cities.

Answers start on page 199.

EXERCISE 13: CHAPTER REVIEW

Directions: Read the following passages and answer the questions, circling the number of the correct answer.

Questions 1–5 are based on the following passage.

> Harriet Hanson was an eleven-year-old girl working in the mill. She later recalled:
>
> I worked in a lower room where I had heard the proposed strike fully, if not vehemently, discussed. I had been an ardent listener to what was said against this attempt at "oppression" on the part of the corporation, and naturally I took sides with the strikers. When the day came on which the girls were to turn out, those in the upper rooms started first, and so many of them left that our mill was at once shut down. Then, when the girls in my room stood irresolute, uncertain what to do . . . I, who began to think they would not go out, after all their talk, became impatient, and started on ahead, saying with childish bravado, "I don't care what you do, I am going to turn out, whether anyone else does or not," and I marched out, and was followed by the others.
>
> As I looked back at the long line that followed me, I was more proud than I have ever been since. . . .

1. The topic of this passage is

    (1) a young girl growing up in a mill town
    (2) the tragedy of child labor
    (3) the rise of the labor movement
    (4) life in the early mills
    (5) a young girl's role in a mill strike

2. Harriet decided to *turn out*. This meant that

    (1) she rearranged her clothes
    (2) she went on strike
    (3) she told the other workers what to do
    (4) she went to the upper rooms
    (5) she converted to Catholicism

3. At first, the girls in Harriet's room stood *irresolute*.
   This meant that they

    (1) were embarrassed by Harriet
    (2) had decided to strike
    (3) had decided to stay at work
    (4) were uncertain about what to do
    (5) were older and wiser than Harriet

4. Harriet spoke with childish *bravado*. She showed

   (1) great confidence and maturity
   (2) a pretense of courage
   (3) a lack of responsibility
   (4) thoughtfulness
   (5) cowardice and fear

5. What happened when Harriet marched out of the mill?

   (1) She was immediately arrested.
   (2) She was fired from her job.
   (3) Her fellow workers followed her.
   (4) She was put in charge of the strike.
   (5) Her co-workers refused to talk to her.

Questions 6–7 are based on the following passage.

It has long been true, and prisoners knew this better than anyone, that the poorer you were, the more likely you were to end up in jail. This was not just because the poor committed more crimes. In fact, they did. The rich did not have to commit crimes to get what they wanted; the laws were on their side. But when the rich did commit crimes, they often were not prosecuted, and if they were they could get out on bail, hire clever lawyers, get better treatment from judges. Somehow, the jails ended up full of poor black people.

6. According to the passage, why do the rich commit fewer crimes than the poor?

   (1) They have a better education and stronger reasoning skills than poor people.
   (2) They tend to be more religious than poor people.
   (3) They can get what they want since the law is on their side.
   (4) They can get out on bail, hire clever lawyers, get better treatment from judges.
   (5) They want to set a good example so that others do not resent their good fortune.

7. What is the main idea of this paragraph?

   (1) The poorer you are, the more likely you are to end up in jail.
   (2) Reform is needed to make the criminal justice system work.
   (3) Rich people can afford to hire clever lawyers and pay bail.
   (4) Poor people commit more crimes than rich people.
   (5) The criminal justice system must become tougher on criminals.

Questions 8–10 are based on the following passage.

In the spring of 1903, I went to Kensington, Pennsylvania, where seventy-five thousand textile workers were on strike. Of this number at least ten thousand were little children. The workers were striking for more pay and shorter hours. Every day little children came into Union Headquarters, some with their hands off, some with the thumb missing, some with their fingers off at the knuckle. They were stooped little things, round-shouldered and skinny. . . .

I asked some of the parents if they would let me have their little boys and girls for a week or ten days, promising to bring them back safe and sound. . . . A man named Sweeny was marshall. . . . A few men and women went with me. . . . The children carried knapsacks on their backs in which was a knife and fork, a tin cup and plate. . . . One little fellow had a drum, and another had a fife. . . . We carried banners that said: . . . "We want time to play. . . ."

. . . Our march had done its work. We had drawn the attention of the nation to the crime of child labor.

8. The children carried

   (1) eating utensils and musical instruments
   (2) knives and forks
   (3) the smaller children
   (4) more pay and shorter hours
   (5) a fife and drum

9. What is this passage about?

   (1) a children's march to protest child labor
   (2) an early fund-raising telethon
   (3) the right of children to play
   (4) the textile workers' strike in Kensington
   (5) the abuse and mutilation of children

10. How many textile workers were on strike in Kensington?

   (1) 10
   (2) 1,903
   (3) 7,000
   (4) 10,000
   (5) 75,000

Answers start on page 200.

CHAPTER REVIEW EVALUATION CHART

Skill	Question Numbers	Review Pages	Number Correct
Finding Details	5, 6, 10	17–22	_____ /3
Words in Context	2, 3, 4	22–27	_____ /3
Restating/ Summarizing	8	27–31	_____ /1
Topic of a Passage	1, 9	32–34	_____ /2
Main Idea of a Paragraph	7	34–36	_____ /1

Your score: _____ out of 10

Passing score: 7 out of 10

CHAPTER 2

CHARTS, GRAPHS, AND MAPS

Charts, graphs, and maps are often used in social studies materials. It is as important for you to understand these illustrations as it is for you to understand reading passages. Illustrations can give detailed information without many words, so they are very helpful to both readers and writers. Can you imagine what it would be like to read or to write the information on a road map in sentences and paragraphs?

Understanding charts, graphs, and maps will help you in future chapters of this book and in your daily life.

CHARTS

WHAT IS A CHART?

A chart is information organized into columns and rows. Another name for a chart is *table*. The purpose of a chart is to allow you to easily locate and compare bits of information. The following example shows the major parts of a chart.

EDUCATION COMPLETED, 1940–1990

Since 1940, the following percentage of Americans aged 25 or over had completed high school or college:

	High School Only	Four or More Years of College
1940	24.5%	4.6%
1950	34.3%	6.2%
1960	41.4%	7.7%
1970	55.2%	11.0%
1980	66.3%	16.3%
1990	77.6%	21.3%

Source: U.S. Bureau of the Census

In the chart above, the title gives the topic. A sentence below the title gives more information about the topic. The information, or **data**, on a chart is organized into rows and columns. A **row** of a chart is all the entries on one horizontal line. In the chart above, each row is labeled by a decade, such as 1940. A **column** consists of all the entries on one vertical line. In the chart above, there are two columns. The column headings are "High School Only" and "Four or More Years of College."

UNDERSTANDING A CHART

Just like a reading passage, every chart has a topic. The title usually tells you what a chart is about. You can often find more clues to the topic of a chart in the headings and sometimes in a subtitle. Look at the chart below.

What is this chart about? _____

THE NATION'S LARGEST CITIES

1990 Rank	1990 Population	Percentage Change Since 1980
1. New York	7,323,000	+3.5%
2. Los Angeles	3,485,000	+17.4%
3. Chicago	2,784,000	−7.4%
4. Houston	1,631,000	+2.2%
5. Philadelphia	1,586,000	−6.1%
6. San Diego	1,111,000	+26.8%
7. Detroit	1,028,000	−14.6%

Source: *Statistical Abstract of the United States, 1993*

The chart is about the percent of population change in the nation's largest cities. You can figure this out by looking at the title and the headings for the columns and rows.

Chart Reading Tip

In order to understand a chart, first read the title and all the headings. Don't try to read the data until you understand what the title and headings are telling you the chart is about.

EXERCISE 1: READING THE TITLES AND HEADINGS ON A CHART

Directions: In your own words, write a sentence telling what each of the following charts is about.

NATIONAL BASKETBALL ASSOCIATION STANDINGS
Atlantic Division

	Wins	Losses	Percentage of Wins	Games Behind
Orlando	18	5	.783	—
New York	16	6	.727	$1\frac{1}{2}$
Miami	12	8	.600	$4\frac{1}{2}$
Boston	11	10	.524	6
Washington	10	10	.500	$6\frac{1}{2}$
New Jersey	9	11	.450	$7\frac{1}{2}$
Philadelphia	3	17	.150	$13\frac{1}{2}$

This chart is about _____

_____

BOCES ADULT LEARNING CENTER BUDGET
ANALYSIS FOR FISCAL YEAR 1996

Budget Item	Amount Recommended
Salaries	$ 298,560
Supplies	12,490
Equipment	26,800
Building	48,000

This chart is about _____

_____

Possible answers start on page 200.

LOCATING DATA ON A CHART

In order to find specific data (bits of information) on a chart, you must use the column and row headings to locate the information you need. The column and row headings label the vertical and horizontal lines of data. In the following chart, the column headings are *1980*, *1990*, and *Percentage Change*. The row headings are the types of foods listed along the left side.

CHANGES IN FOOD CONSUMPTION, 1980–1990 (pounds per person)			
	1980	**1990**	**Percentage Change**
Dairy products	543.2	569.7	+ 4.6%
Red meat	126.4	112.4	−11.1%
Flour and cereal products	144.5	183.5	+26.9%
Fats and oils	57.2	62.2	+ 8.7%

Source: U.S. Department of Agriculture

The data in the chart above can be used to help us understand how the American diet changed from 1980 to 1990. Answer the following sample questions based on the chart.

▶ What was the number of pounds of red meat consumed by the average American in 1990?_____

First look for the row labeled *Red meat*. Then look for the column labeled *1990*. If you draw imaginary lines across from *Red meat* and down from *1990*, the place where the lines cross is the number you are looking for. The average American ate 112.4 pounds of red meat in 1990.

▶ Of the items listed, which food had the greatest percentage change in consumption from 1980 to 1990? _____

You must look for the largest number in the *Percentage Change* column. That number is 26.9%. Looking across the row, you find that flour and cereal products had the greatest percentage change of the items listed.

▶ Did the consumption of dairy products increase or decrease from 1980 to 1990? _____

To answer this question, you could compare two numbers. Consumption of dairy products for 1980 is 543.2. For 1990, it is 569.7. Since the 1990 number is higher, the consumption of dairy products increased. You could also look in the "percentage change" column to find the answer to this question. The plus sign in that column tells you that consumption increased.

▶ By how many pounds did the consumption of flour and cereal products increase from 1980 to 1990? _____

In order to find the amount of the increase, first find the amount of consumption in 1980 and in 1990. Consumption of flour and cereal products was 144.5 pounds in 1980 and 183.5 pounds in 1990. To find the increase, you need to find the difference between the two numbers, so you subtract: 183.5 – 144.5 = 39.

Chart Reading Tip

If you are asked to find an increase, look for numbers or percentages that become larger over time. When you see a plus (+) sign, such as +18%, the plus sign tells you there was an increase of 18%. If you are asked to find a decrease, look for numbers that become smaller over time. When you see a minus (–) sign, such as –18%, the minus sign tells you there was a decrease of 18%.

EXERCISE 2: FINDING INFORMATION ON A CHART

Directions: Use the information in the chart below to answer the questions at the top of page 51.

CHANGES IN FOOD CONSUMPTION, 1980–1990 (pounds per capita)			
	1980	**1990**	**Percentage Change**
Fresh vegetables	92.5	113.3	+22.5%
Sugar and other sweeteners	123.9	140.7	+13.6%
Fresh fruits	86.9	92.2	+ 6.1%
Poultry	40.6	55.9	+37.7%
Eggs	271.0	233.0	–14.0%
Fish and shellfish	12.4	15.0	+21.0%
Coffee	10.3	10.3	+ 0 %

Source: U.S. Department of Agriculture

1. How many pounds of eggs did the average American consume in 1980?

   _____

2. In 1990, the average American ate 15 pounds of

   _____

3. Between 1980 and 1990, Americans decreased their consumption of

   _____

4. How did the consumption of coffee in 1990 compare with the consumption of coffee in 1980?

   _____

5. By what percentage did the consumption of sweeteners increase between 1980 and 1990?

   _____

6. Americans increased their consumption of many foods between 1980 and 1990. What category increased by the greatest percentage?

   _____

Answers start on page 200.

FINDING THE MAIN IDEA OF A CHART

Like a reading passage, a chart may illustrate a main idea. The author may be trying to make a central point by choosing and displaying data a certain way. When you study a chart, ask yourself what the chart is telling you and what its purpose is. Then think of a way the data could be summarized in one main idea statement.

Sometimes the main idea of a chart will be stated directly in the title or subtitle. Other times you must find the main idea by looking at the headings or by studying the data.

Chart Reading Tip

Because data are easier to read and compare in smaller numbers, charts that compare large numbers often use phrases such as *in thousands* in their subtitle or key. *In thousands* means that each number listed in the chart is really 1,000 times that number. So, for example, the number *18* on a chart that says *in thousands* actually means *18,000*.

GAINERS AND LOSERS
Union Membership (in thousands)

	1975	1985	1993
United Steel Workers	1,062	572	421
International Ladies' Garment Workers Union	363	210	133
Communications Workers of America	476	524	472
National Alliance of Letter Carriers	151	186	210
Service Employees International Union	490	688	919

Source: AFL-CIO

Study the chart "Gainers and Losers." Read the title, subtitle, and headings. Then look carefully at the data to see what the chart is illustrating. Ask yourself what the chart is telling you and what its purpose could be.

Following are four choices for the main idea. Circle the number of the choice that accurately summarizes the data for the chart. What is the main idea of this chart?

(1) The largest unions have thousands of members.
(2) In the last eight years, the International Ladies' Garment Workers Union lost almost half its members.
(3) While most unions lost members over the last eighteen years, some have gained members.
(4) In life, there are always gainers and losers.

You were correct if you circled (3). Of the five unions listed, three have lost members over the last eighteen years, while two have gained members. The chart makes clear that the "gainers and losers" are the various unions.

While choice (1) is a true statement that is supported by the data, it is not the main point of the chart, which shows the *changes* in union membership over time. Choice (2) is also a detail, not the main idea. Choice (4) is a general statement that does not refer to the data at all.

EXERCISE 3: MAIN IDEA OF A CHART

Directions: After each chart are five choices for main idea. Choose the one that accurately summarizes the data on the chart.

EARNINGS: SEX AND OCCUPATIONS			
For every $1,000 made by men in these occupations during 1993, women received the following amounts.			
Managers	$667	Security guards	$796
Doctors and lawyers	$765	Farmers/fishers	$883
Technicians	$761	Construction workers	$821
Salespeople	$605	Machine operators/ inspectors	$698
Administrative assistants/ secretaries	$762	Truckers/drivers	$785
Service workers	$893	Laborers	$897

Source: U.S. Bureau of Labor Statistics

1. What is the main idea of this chart?

   (1) Traditionally male occupations are now being filled by women.
   (2) Women earn less than men in the same occupations.
   (3) In most occupations, men are worth more than women.
   (4) It costs more to hire a man than it does a woman.
   (5) Women's and men's salaries are finally becoming equal.

UNDERGRADUATE DEGREES AWARDED TO WOMEN

	1971	1991	Percentage Change
Engineering	0.8%	13.9%	+1,637.5%
Agriculture	4.2%	32.7%	+ 678.6%
Business	9.1%	47.2%	+ 418.7%
Computer science	13.6%	29.3%	+ 115.4%
Psychology	44.5%	72.6%	+ 63.1%
Social sciences	36.8%	45.1%	+ 22.6%
Education	74.5%	78.9%	+ 5.9%

Source: U.S. National Center for Education Statistics

2. What is the main idea of this chart?

   (1) In many areas, the number of women earning undergraduate degrees increased from 1971 to 1991.
   (2) An increasing number of women are getting degrees in engineering.
   (3) Women are going after men's jobs with increasing success.
   (4) Women obtained higher salaries in 1991 than they did in 1971 because they have attained a higher education level.
   (5) Education is still the most female-dominated undergraduate degree, although Psychology is a close second.

Answers start on page 200.

GRAPHS

A graph allows a reader to spot trends, make comparisons, and draw conclusions from data. Being able to read graphs will help you in many practical situations as well as in social studies. In this part of the chapter, you will look at four types of graphs: pictographs, bar graphs, line graphs, and circle graphs.

FINDING THE TOPIC OF A GRAPH

Like a chart, every graph has a topic. The title usually tells you the topic of the graph. Sometimes there is also a subtitle to help you out. Read the titles and then check the other information on the graph, such as the labels and the data, to make sure you have an accurate idea of the topic of the graph.

Look at the sample graph below. What is the topic of this graph?

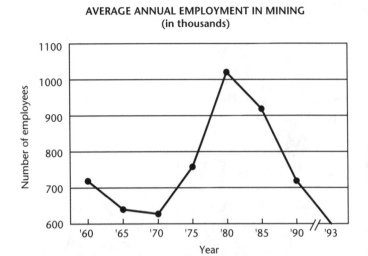

AVERAGE ANNUAL EMPLOYMENT IN MINING
(in thousands)

Source: U.S. Bureau of Labor Statistics

This graph shows the average annual employment in mining. The title of this graph tells you what the graph is about.

EXERCISE 4: TOPIC OF A GRAPH

Directions: In the space provided, write the topic of the following graphs. Study the titles and other information on each graph carefully before writing.

Graph 1

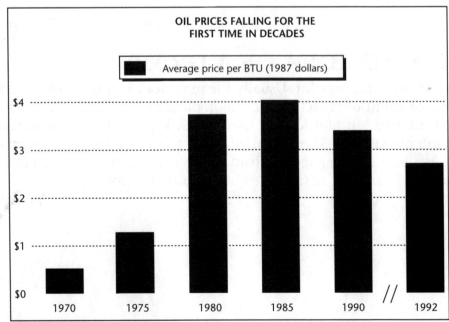

OIL PRICES FALLING FOR THE FIRST TIME IN DECADES

Average price per BTU (1987 dollars)

Source: U.S. Energy Information Administration

topic: _____

Graph 2

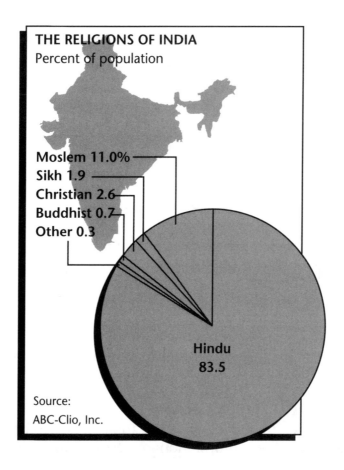

THE RELIGIONS OF INDIA
Percent of population

Moslem 11.0%
Sikh 1.9
Christian 2.6
Buddhist 0.7
Other 0.3

Hindu
83.5

Source:
ABC-Clio, Inc.

topic: _____

Possible answers start on page 201.

THE MAIN IDEA OF A GRAPH

Graphs illustrate a point. Usually the main idea will be stated directly in the title or subtitle. To determine the main idea, read the titles and other written information and look at the data. Ask yourself, "What message is the graph giving me?" Then think of a way to summarize the information.

Study the graph on page 57. Read the title, the scale, and the labels and look at the data. Then answer the questions that follow it.

UNEMPLOYMENT RATE—1994
(in percent)

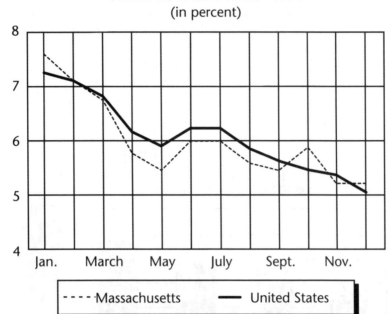

1. What is the graph about? _____

2. Why are there two lines on the graph? _____

3. The main idea of this graph is that
    (1) the unemployment rates in Massachusetts and the United States generally rose and fell together
    (2) the unemployment rate in the United States peaked at about 7% and then dropped
    (3) the unemployment rate in Massachusetts dipped as low as 5.2% from a high of 7.6%
    (4) Massachusetts's high school dropout rate is lower than the national average
    (5) Massachusetts had the lowest unemployment rate in the nation

Be sure you tried to answer all the questions above. Then read the following explanations of the correct answers.

1. The topic of the graph is *1994 unemployment rates in the United States and Massachusetts*. You know this by looking at the title and the labels for the two lines.

2. There are two lines because two things are being compared. One line stands for the United States as a whole, and the other line stands for the state of Massachusetts.

3. Choice (1) is correct because it describes the relationship between the two lines. Choices (2) and (3) deal with only one of the two lines. Choice (4) has nothing to do with the graph. Choice (5) is related to the graph, but the graph does not show data for other states.

EXERCISE 5: THE MAIN IDEA OF A GRAPH

Directions: This exercise is based on two graphs. Before you answer any of the questions about a graph, read the titles and the other written information and look at the data. Ask yourself what message the graph might be trying to give you and what its purpose might be.

   After each graph are "warm-up" questions to help you understand the graph and then five choices for main idea. Answer the "warm-up" questions in your own words. Then choose the number of the correct choice for the main idea of each graph.

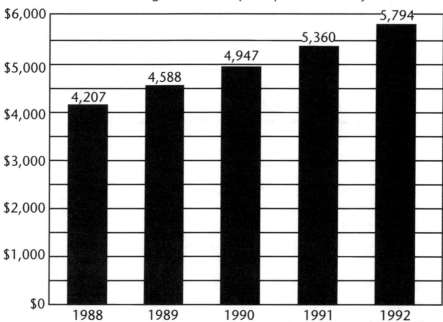

RISING HOSPITAL COSTS
According to the American Hospital Association,
Average Cost to Hospitals per Patient Stay

Source: American Hospital Association

1. What is the topic of this graph? _____

_____

2. What trend do you see when you look at the height of the bars changing over time? (A trend is a general direction or pattern of development.)

_____

3. What is the main idea of the graph?
   (1) The rate of increase of hospital costs is slowing down.
   (2) Hospital costs increased each year from 1988 to 1992.
   (3) Hospital costs peaked in 1992.
   (4) The high cost of a hospital stay makes health insurance a necessity.
   (5) High hospital costs are a national scandal.

**PERSONAL BUDGET OF A
TYPICAL WELFARE RECIPIENT**

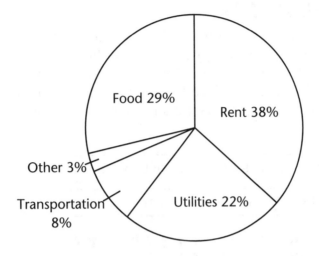

4. What is the topic of this graph? _____

_____

5. The graph shows that, in general, welfare recipients spend most of their
money on three things. What are they? _____

_____

6. What is the main idea of this graph?

   (1) Welfare recipients spend a great deal of their income on rent.
   (2) Welfare reform is long overdue.
   (3) Welfare recipients spend most of their money on necessities.
   (4) Welfare recipients do not manage their money wisely.
   (5) When people have to spend most of their income on food, rent,
   and energy, they go on welfare.

Answers start on page 201.

READING DATA ON A GRAPH

FINDING INFORMATION ON A PICTOGRAPH

A *pictograph* uses symbols to display information. In order to find specific details on a pictograph, you must use the key. The key tells you what the pictures on the graph stand for. For example, look at the following pictograph. Each picture, or symbol, stands for 50 prisoners per 100,000 people. Find the number of prisoners per 100,000 people in Delaware.

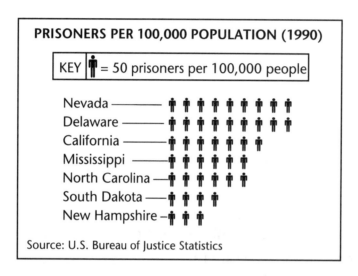

Find the row labeled Delaware. There are nine symbols. The key tells you that each symbol stands for 50 prisoners. Multiply: 9 × 50 = 450. There are about 450 prisoners per 100,000 people in Delaware.

Look again at the pictograph in the example and answer the following questions.

▶ Which states had the highest number of prisoners per 100,000 people?

_____

To find the states with the highest number of prisoners per 100,000 people, you must find the longest rows of symbols. Those rows are labeled *Nevada* and *Delaware*.

▶ Which state had the lowest number of prisoners per 100,000 people?

_____

To find the state with the lowest number of prisoners per 100,000 people, you must find the shortest row. That row is labeled *New Hampshire*.

▶ Which state has more prisoners per 100,000 population, Mississippi or California? _____

California has more. California's row has seven symbols, and Mississippi's has only six.

Graph Reading Tip
Pictographs are used to make general comparisons. The information on a pictograph is not exact.

EXERCISE 6: READING PICTOGRAPHS
Directions: Fill in the blanks with the correct information based on each graph.

CITY TAXES PER PERSON

KEY $ = $100

New York	$ $ $ $ $ $ $ $
San Antonio	$
San Francisco	$ $ $ $
Washington, D.C.	$ $ $ $ $ $ $ $ $ $ $ $ $
New Orleans	$ $

Source: *U/S A Statistical Portrait of the American People*

1. What were the approximate taxes per person in New Orleans? _____

2. Which city had the highest taxes per person? _____

3. Which city had the lowest taxes per person? _____

4. Which city's per-person taxes are lower, San Francisco's or New York's? _____

5. What is the main idea of the pictograph "City Taxes per Person"?
   (1) Washington, D.C., is one of the most expensive cities in the country to live in.
   (2) San Antonio and New Orleans have very low city taxes.
   (3) Cities that bring in a lot of tax money are able to provide more services to the public.
   (4) Per-person city taxes in the United States can range from $100 to $1,300.
   (5) City taxes in San Francisco are reasonable, so most people could afford to live there.

Answers start on page 201.

READING BAR GRAPHS

A *bar graph* uses bars to display information. Like a pictograph, a bar graph is a way to compare information quickly and easily. The information is not exact, but you can make good estimates from a bar graph. Study the following bar graph. In order to find specific facts on a bar graph, you must use the scale to read the height of the bars. What is the average life expectancy for women in the United States?

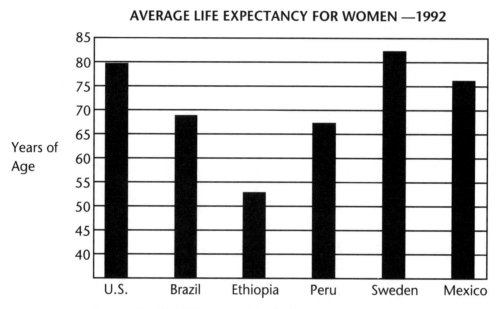

AVERAGE LIFE EXPECTANCY FOR WOMEN —1992

Source: *The World Almanac and Book of Facts*

In order to find the average life expectancy for women in the United States, first you must find the bar labeled *U.S.* Now draw an imaginary horizontal line from the top end of the bar over to the scale. Then either read the number on the scale or, if the line is between two scale entries, estimate the number. In this case, the average life expectancy of women in the U.S. is slightly below 80. A good estimate would be 79 years.

▶ Use the bar graph in the example above to answer the following questions.

▶ What nation had the shortest life expectancy for women? _____

To find the nation with the shortest life expectancy, find the shortest bar. At the bottom of the bar is the name of the country, Ethiopia.

Only one nation on the graph had a life expectancy for women higher than that of the U.S. Which country was that ? _____

To find the nation with a life expectancy higher than that of the U.S., find the U.S. bar. Now draw an imaginary horizontal line across the graph even with the top end of the U.S. bar. You will find that only one bar ends above the line. At the bottom of that bar is the name of the country, Sweden.

Graph Reading Tip

In multiple-choice questions based on graphs, you can eliminate wrong choices. Since you are usually expected to make estimates based on graphs, there should be one answer choice that is closest to your estimate.

EXERCISE 7: READING BAR GRAPHS

Directions: Fill in the blanks with the correct information from the graph. Estimate the answer if you cannot read an exact figure from the graph.

AVERAGE LIFE EXPECTANCY FOR MEN —1992

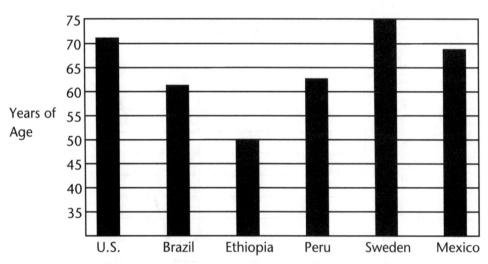

Source: *The World Almanac and Book of Facts*

1. Which nation had an average life expectancy for men of sixty-eight years? _____

2. What was the average life expectancy for men in Ethiopia? _____

3. Which nation had the longest life expectancy for men? _____

4. Which nation had the shortest life expectancy for men? _____

5. How many nations on the graph had a shorter life expectancy for men than the United States? _____

6. About how many more years does the average man in Sweden live than the average man in Ethiopia? _____

Answers start on page 201.

READING LINE GRAPHS

A *line graph* is similar to a bar graph in many ways. However, instead of using bars, lines connect different points (called *data points*). Line graphs are used to show trends or developments. On the side of a line graph is a **vertical scale**. Along the bottom of a line graph is a **horizontal scale**. To read a line graph, you read up from the horizontal scale and across from the vertical scale to a particular point on the line.

Line graphs are easier to understand if you carefully read the titles and other words on the graph before you try reading the data. Study the following line graph and answer the question, "What was the population of London in 1800?"

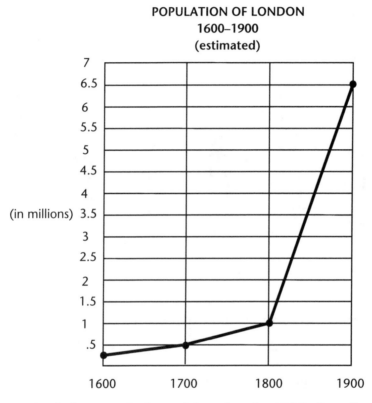

POPULATION OF LONDON
1600–1900
(estimated)

In order to find the population of London in 1800, first find *1800* on the horizontal scale (along the bottom of the graph). Now go straight up until you reach the data point for 1800. Now go straight across to the left until you reach the vertical scale. At the height of the data point, the closest number on the vertical scale is 1. That means that the population of London in 1800 was about 1 million.

Use the line graph in the example above to answer the following questions.

▶ In what year shown on the graph did London have the smallest population? _____

Find the lowest data point on the line. Look straight down to the horizontal scale and find the date of that point. London had its smallest population in 1600.

▶ In what year shown on the graph did London have its largest population? _____

Look at the line and find the highest point on it. Looking down to the horizontal scale, you find the year 1900. Therefore, London had its largest population in 1900.

▶ Between 1600 and 1900, what happened to the size of London's population? _____

Look at the first point on the line, the shape of the line, and the endpoint of the line. The population of London increased greatly during the period, from less than half a million people to 6.5 million.

To summarize or see a trend on a line graph, look at the whole line and get a general idea of what happened to the data over the time shown.

EXERCISE 8: READING LINE GRAPHS

Directions: Answer the questions based on the following graph. If you can't read an exact answer from the graph, estimate.

AMERICA MOVES TO THE CITIES
Percent of U.S. Population Living in Urban Areas

Source: U.S. Bureau of the Census

1. In what year shown on the graph was the percentage of urban population the lowest? _____

2. In what year shown on the graph was the percentage of urban population the highest? _____

3. What percentage of the population of the United States lived in urban areas in 1960? _____

4. Which of the following best describes the trend shown by this line graph?

   (1) The percentage of people living in urban areas of the United States has steadily fallen.
   (2) The percentage of people living in rural areas of the United States has steadily increased.
   (3) The percentage of people living in a few major cities in the United States has risen steadily.
   (4) In 1910, most people lived in the northeastern United States, but by 1980 the population was shifting south and west.
   (5) The percentage of people living in urban areas of the United States rose steadily and then leveled off.

Answers start on page 201.

READING CIRCLE GRAPHS

A circle graph uses parts, or segments, of a circle to display information. Think of the circle graph as a pie. The segments look like slices of the pie. The size of the segment tells how much of the whole it represents.

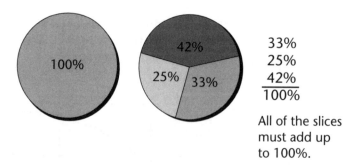

33%
25%
42%
‾‾‾‾‾
100%

All of the slices must add up to 100%.

On the following graph, each segment has a label to tell you what it stands for. Find what percent of the U.S. population earned between $15,000 and $20,000.

DISTRIBUTION OF FAMILY INCOME—1980

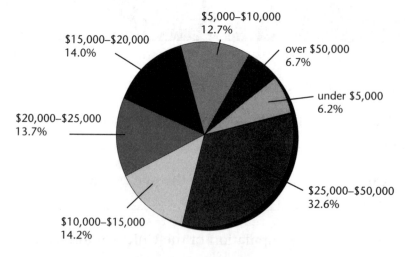

Source: U/S A Statistical Portrait of the American People

First find the segment labeled *$15,000–$20,000*. The percentage *14.0%* is written just below the label of the segment. Sometimes the label and percentage are written in the segment. Other times, especially when the segment is very small, they may be connected to the segment by a line.

Use the circle graph "Distribution of Family Income" to answer the following sample questions.

▶ The largest percentage of families in 1980 were at what income level? _____

Find the largest segment—32.6%. It is labeled *$25,000–$50,000*.

▶ In 1980, 12.7% of families were at what income level? _____

Look for the segment marked *12.7%*. Read the label of that segment: *$5,000–$10,000*.

EXERCISE 9: READING CIRCLE GRAPHS

Directions: Fill in the blanks with the correct information based on each graph.

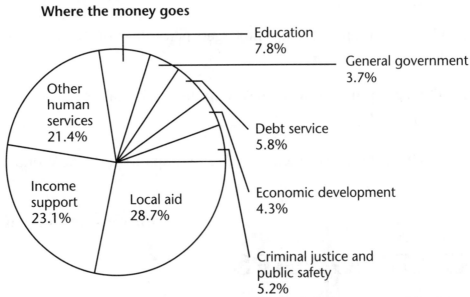

THE STATE BUDGET
Where the money goes

1. What percent of the state budget pays for education?

   _____

2. In what area does the state government spend the most money?

   _____

3. What expense uses up exactly 4.3% percent of the state budget?

   _____

4. Does the state spend more money on education or on criminal justice and public safety? _____

POPULATION BY AGE GROUP IN THE CITY OF SADDLETOP

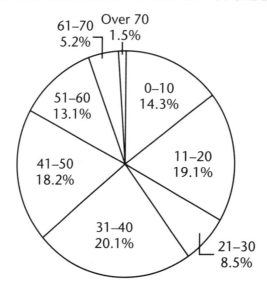

5. What age group makes up the smallest percentage of the population?

   _____

6. What age group makes up the largest percentage of the population?

   _____

7. What age group below 60 makes up the smallest percentage of the population? _____

8. Which age group is larger, the 11–20 group or the 41–50 group?

   _____

Answers start on page 201.

READING MAPS

WHAT ARE MAPS?

"Excuse me, sir, could you help me find 838 Catalpa Drive?"

"No problem. Just continue up Franklin Avenue and make a right at the gas station. You will then be on Woodcliff Drive. One block up, the road forks. Take the left fork. You are now on Shelburne Drive. Continue on Shelburne until you bear right at the next fork . . ."

"I'm sorry. You've lost me. I just can't picture where I'm supposed to be going."

"Let me draw you a map. Then it should be clearer."

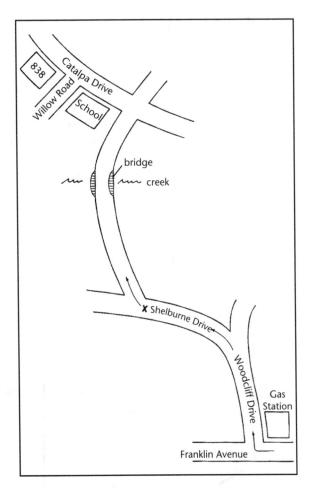

It is easier to follow directions when you use a map. See if you can find the gas station described in the directions. Now find the fork on Woodcliff Drive where Shelburne Drive splits off. Follow Shelburne Drive to where it forks.

Use the map to finish writing directions to 838 Catalpa Drive. Start at the *X* on the map and use landmarks whenever you can.

_____

_____

Your directions should be something like this: Take the right fork. Go straight over a bridge above a small creek. On your left you will see a school. Turn left at the school. You will then be on Catalpa Drive. Continue on Catalpa Drive past Willow Road. On the left you'll find 838 Catalpa Drive.

A **map** is a drawing of the surface of a region. A map could represent the entire earth, a continent, or a nation. Or, as in the above example, it can represent an area as small as your own neighborhood.

There are different kinds of maps for different purposes. In this chapter, you will be looking at common parts of maps, including directions, distances, keys, and borders between states and countries. You will then be able to practice reading different kinds of maps.

DIRECTION AND DISTANCE

Different kinds of information are found on a map. There are important symbols on a map that help orient us to it and see how the places shown on a map fit together. Following is a map of the Baltimore area. The direction symbol in the upper right corner of the map shows that the top of the map is *north*. This means that places near the top of the map are north of things lower down on the map. If you know north you can figure out the other directions.

If north is toward the top of the map, *south* is toward the bottom. *East* is to the right, and *west* is to the left.

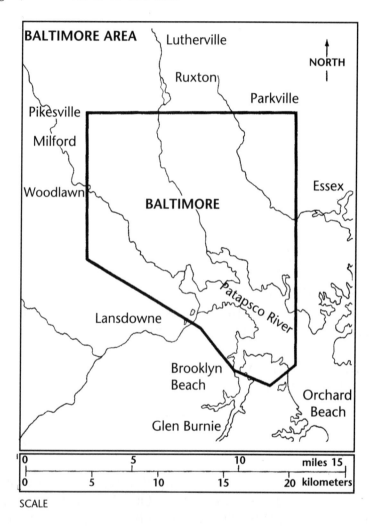

▶ Lutherville is straight north of Baltimore. Name a town that is straight

east of Baltimore. _____

East is to the right. Therefore, look to the right of Baltimore. The town of Essex is east of Baltimore.

At the bottom of the map is a **scale** in miles (and kilometers). You can use the scale to estimate distances. The easiest way to use a scale is to mark off the distance between two places on the edge of a piece of paper. Then put the edge of the paper next to the scale to estimate the distance.

▶ About how many miles is it from Baltimore's west boundary near Woodlawn directly across town to its east boundary?

On the edge of a piece of paper, mark off the distance from the west boundary near Woodlawn straight across to the east boundary. Now line up the left marking for the west boundary with the zero on the scale at the bottom of the map. Your right marking for the east boundary should hit the scale at a little less than 10 miles. Now you know it is a little less than 10 miles from the west boundary to the east boundary of Baltimore.

EXERCISE 10: DIRECTION AND DISTANCE ON A MAP

Directions: Answer the following questions based on the map of Cambodia.

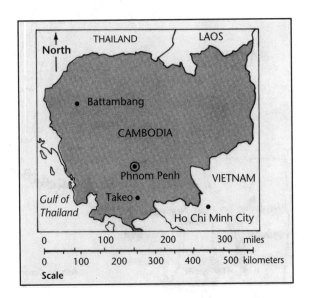

1. Which two nations are north of Cambodia?

   _____

2. What direction must you travel to go from Phnom Penh to Takeo? _____

3. Approximately how many miles is it from Battambang to Phnom Penh? _____

4. If you travel south from Battambang, what body of water will you reach? _____

5. Approximately how many miles is it from Phnom Penh to Ho Chi Minh City in Vietnam? _____

Answers start on page 202.

USING A MAP KEY

Most maps have keys. A map key defines the various symbols used on a map. A key can define different kinds of boundary lines such as international and state boundaries. It can give symbols for cities of varying sizes and for capital cities. It can identify symbols that represent vegetation, climate, population, and economic products.

The following is a map of New England, a region in the northeastern United States. Look at the key to find the symbol for state capitals.

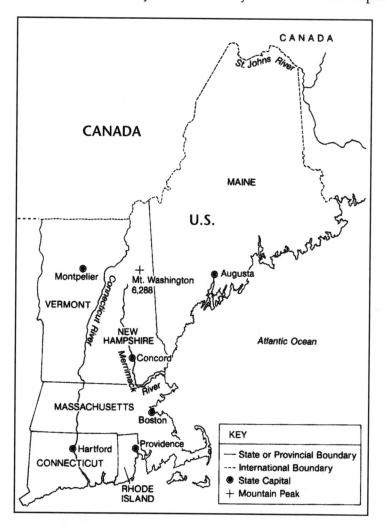

▶ What is the state capital of Connecticut? _____

Looking at the key, you find that ⦿ is the symbol for state capitals. Find the state of Connecticut on the map. Now look for the symbol ⦿ within the state. The symbol is labeled *Hartford*, which is the capital of Connecticut.

Look again at the key to determine what kind of line is used for the international boundary between Canada and the United States.

▶ What river is part of that international boundary? _____

The key tells you that the international boundary is marked by a dotted line.

Following the dotted line, only one river is part of that boundary, the St. Johns River between Maine and Canada.

▶ The only mountain peak marked on this map is Mt. Washington, the highest peak in New England. In what state is Mt. Washington located?

_____

The key tells you that the symbol for a mountain is +. Looking for the symbol + on the map, you should be able to locate Mt. Washington, which is in the state of New Hampshire.

EXERCISE 11: USING A MAP KEY

Directions: Brazil is one of the largest countries in the world. It is in South America. Use the map of Brazil to answer the following questions. For some of the questions, you will have to use the key.

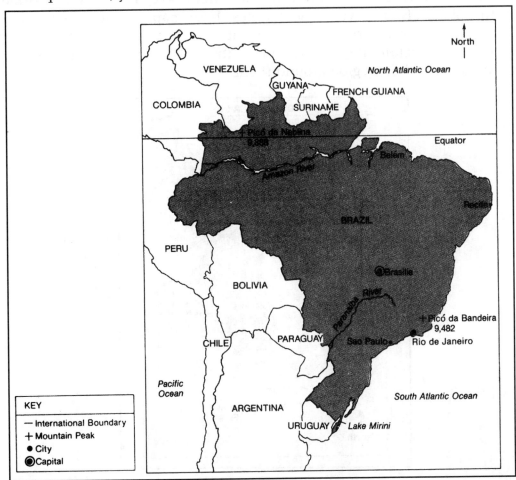

1. A major geographical feature of Brazil is a very famous river that runs across the northern part of the country. What is the name of the river?

_____

2. Part of the southernmost tip of Brazil is a lake. What is the name of the lake? _____

3. With what other country does Brazil share the lake at its southern tip?

_____

4. What is the capital of Brazil? _____

5. The mouth of a river is where it enters the ocean. The mouth of the Amazon River is near what special line that crosses the map?

_____

6. What is the name of the highest mountain peak in Brazil?

_____

Answers start on page 202.

HISTORICAL MAPS

Historical maps can help us understand the past. They can show political boundaries of a past time period. They also can be used to illustrate historical trends and events. Sometimes these maps of the past can also help us make sense of the present. Look at the following map of the eastern United States before the American Revolution. What nation controlled the Great Lakes and the region around them?

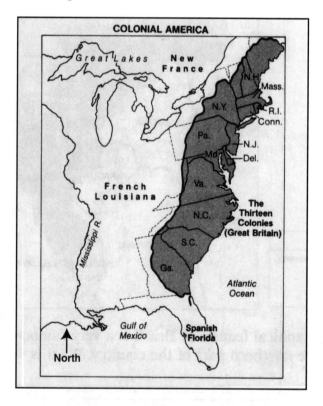

In order to find what nation controlled the Great Lakes area, first find the Great Lakes on the map. The area north and east of the Great Lakes is called *New France*. The area south and west of the lakes is called *French Louisiana*. So you know that the whole region was controlled by France.

Look again at the map of the thirteen colonies on page 74 and answer the following questions.

▶ What nation controlled New York (N.Y.)? _____

Find New York (N.Y.) on the map. It was one of the thirteen colonies controlled by Great Britain.

▶ What nation controlled Florida? _____

Florida was called *Spanish Florida,* so you know it was controlled by Spain.

EXERCISE 12: READING HISTORICAL MAPS

Directions: Answer the questions based on the following map.

NATIVE AMERICANS OF NORTH AMERICA

1. The Pawnee were part of which group of Native Americans?

    (1) Inuit (Eskimo) and Aleut
    (2) Eastern Forests Indians
    (3) Plains Indians
    (4) Northwest Coast Indians
    (5) Southwest Indians

2. The far north of the continent was inhabited by which group or groups?

   (1) Inuit (Eskimo) and Aleut
   (2) Eastern Forests Indians
   (3) Plains Indians
   (4) Northwest Coast Indians
   (5) Southwest Indians

3. Which of the following tribes was Southwest Indians?

   (1) Cree
   (2) Paiute
   (3) Cherokee
   (4) Sioux
   (5) Hopi

Answers start on page 202.

EXERCISE 13: CHAPTER REVIEW

Directions: Study each illustration carefully, then choose the correct answer.

Questions 1–3 are based on the following chart.

RATING COMPARABLE JOBS
How state of Washington determines what a job demands

In number of points	Secretary 1 steno	Electrician	Clerk-typist 1	Truck driver 1	Registered nurse 1
Knowledge and skills	122	122	106	61	280
Mental demands	30	30	26	10	122
Accountability	35	30	35	13	160
Working conditions	0	15	0	13	11
Total job points	187	197	167	97	573
Annual salary	$17,108	$25,404	$13,468	$20,856	$20,440

1. Which job earns the highest annual salary?

    (1) secretary
    (2) electrician
    (3) clerk-typist
    (4) truck driver
    (5) registered nurse

2. Which job was given the highest number of points for knowledge and skills?

    (1) secretary
    (2) electrician
    (3) clerk-typist
    (4) truck driver
    (5) registered nurse

3. Truck driving was given how many total job points?

    (1) 10
    (2) 13
    (3) 61
    (4) 97
    (5) 197

Questions 4–5 are based on the following pictograph.

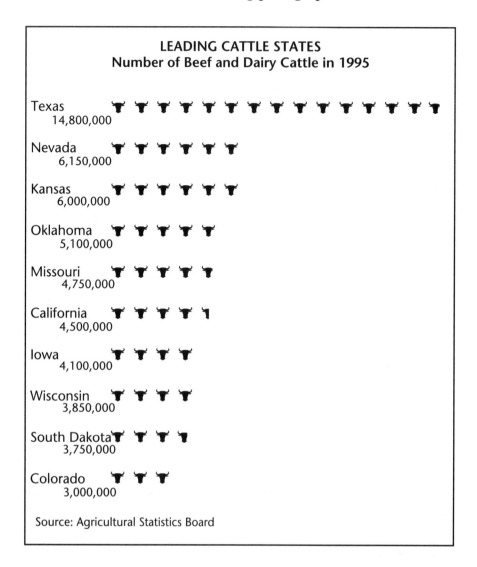

LEADING CATTLE STATES
Number of Beef and Dairy Cattle in 1995

Texas
14,800,000

Nevada
6,150,000

Kansas
6,000,000

Oklahoma
5,100,000

Missouri
4,750,000

California
4,500,000

Iowa
4,100,000

Wisconsin
3,850,000

South Dakota
3,750,000

Colorado
3,000,000

Source: Agricultural Statistics Board

4. Which state had the most beef and dairy cattle in 1995?

    (1) Texas
    (2) California
    (3) Alaska
    (4) Colorado
    (5) Nevada

5. Which state ranked third in total number of beef and dairy cattle in 1995?

    (1) Texas
    (2) California
    (3) Kansas
    (4) Wisconsin
    (5) Colorado

Questions 6–7 are based on the following bar graph.

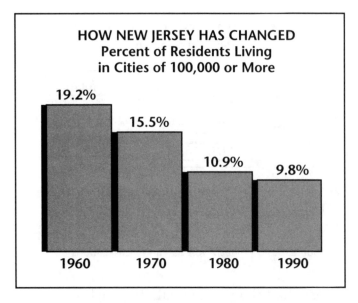

HOW NEW JERSEY HAS CHANGED
Percent of Residents Living
in Cities of 100,000 or More

19.2% — 1960
15.5% — 1970
10.9% — 1980
9.8% — 1990

6. What is the main idea of this bar graph?

    (1) New Jersey has changed.
    (2) Over a thirty-year period, a declining number of Americans lived in cities of over 100,000.
    (3) New Jersey's population declined between 1960 and 1990.
    (4) An increasing percentage of New Jersey residents live in cities of 100,000 or more.
    (5) The percentage of New Jersey residents living in cities of 100,000 or more declined between 1960 and 1990.

7. What percent of New Jersey residents lived in cities of 100,000 or more in 1970?

    (1) 19.2%
    (2) 18.3%
    (3) 15.5%
    (4) 10.9%
    (5) 9.8%

Questions 8–9 are based on the following line graph.

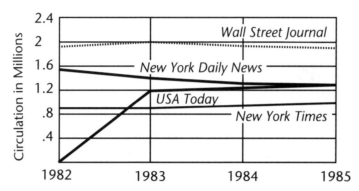

USA TODAY VS. THE COMPETITION
Paid Circulation

Source: *Boston Globe*/Audit Bureau of Circulations

8. Which two papers had the same circulation in 1985?

    (1) *New York Times* and *USA Today*
    (2) *Wall Street Journal* and *New York Daily News*
    (3) *New York Times* and *Wall Street Journal*
    (4) *USA Today* and *Wall Street Journal*
    (5) *New York Daily News* and *USA Today*

9. What was the circulation of the *Wall Street Journal* at the beginning of 1983?

    (1) 1,200
    (2) 2,000
    (3) 2,400
    (4) 2,000,000
    (5) 2,400,000

Questions 10–12 are based on the following circle graph.

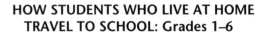

**HOW STUDENTS WHO LIVE AT HOME
TRAVEL TO SCHOOL: Grades 1–6**

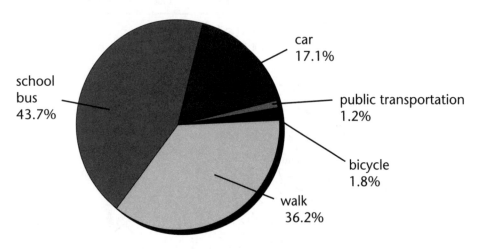

Source: *U/S A Statistical Portrait of the American People*

10. The main idea of this circle graph is
    (1) most Americans oppose school busing and send their children to
    school by other means
    (2) nobody walks to school anymore
    (3) most elementary school children ride a school bus to school
    regularly
    (4) most children in grades 1–6 get to school by walking, school bus,
    or car
    (5) bicycles are becoming more popular for traveling to school

11. What percent of children in grades 1–6 travel to school by car?
    (1) 1.2%
    (2) 1.8%
    (3) 17.1%
    (4) 36.2%
    (5) 43.7%

12. 43.7 percent of students in grades 1–6 travel to school by what means?
    (1) walking
    (2) school bus
    (3) car
    (4) bicycle
    (5) public transportation

Questions 13–14 are based on the following map.

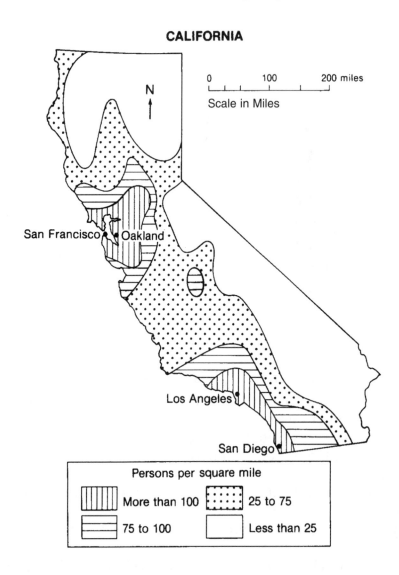

CALIFORNIA

13. What is the population density of the area within 25 miles of San Francisco?

    (1) less than 10
    (2) less than 25
    (3) 25 to 75
    (4) 75 to 100
    (5) more than 100

14. If you drove 200 miles straight north from San Diego and stopped, what would be the population density of the area you stopped in?

    (1) less than 25
    (2) 25 to 75
    (3) 75 to 100
    (4) more than 100
    (5) more than 500

Questions 15–17 are based on the following map.

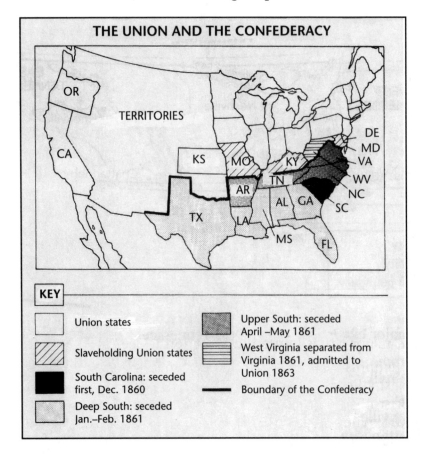

THE UNION AND THE CONFEDERACY

KEY

□ Union states

▨ Slaveholding Union states

■ South Carolina: seceded first, Dec. 1860

▨ Deep South: seceded Jan.–Feb. 1861

▨ Upper South: seceded April –May 1861

☰ West Virginia separated from Virginia 1861, admitted to Union 1863

— Boundary of the Confederacy

15. Which state seceded first from the Union?

    (1) West Virginia
    (2) Missouri
    (3) South Carolina
    (4) Virginia
    (5) Georgia

16. Which of the following states was a slaveholding Union state?

    (1) Kansas
    (2) Kentucky
    (3) Texas
    (4) Arkansas
    (5) California

17. What did Texas do during the Civil War?

    (1) It was a Union state that banned slavery.
    (2) It remained a slaveholding Union State.
    (3) It seceded from the Union in December 1860.
    (4) It seceded from the Union in January or February of 1861.
    (5) It seceded from the Union in April or May of 1861.

Questions 18–20 are based on the following map.

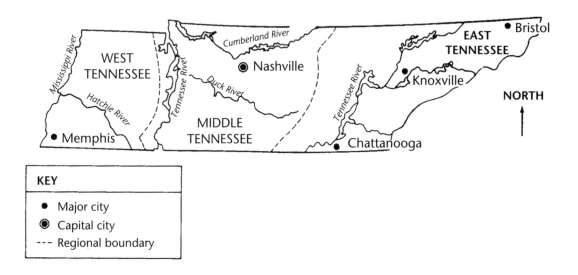

18. What major city is located in West Tennessee?

    (1) Memphis
    (2) Nashville
    (3) Bristol
    (4) Knoxville
    (5) Chattanooga

19. What major city is located on the Tennessee River directly east of the state capital?

    (1) Memphis
    (2) Nashville
    (3) Bristol
    (4) Knoxville
    (5) Chattanooga

20. What river forms the western border of the state?

    (1) the Hatchie River
    (2) the Tennessee River
    (3) the Duck River
    (4) the Cumberland River
    (5) the Mississippi River

Answers start on page 202.

CHAPTER REVIEW EVALUATION CHART

Skill	Question Numbers	Review Pages	Number Correct
Reading a Chart	1, 2, 3	46–51	_____ /3
Main Idea of a Graph	6, 10	54–59	_____ /2
Reading a Pictograph	4, 5	60–61	_____ /2
Reading a Bar Graph	7	62–63	_____ /1
Reading a Line Graph	8, 9	64–66	_____ /2
Reading a Circle Graph	11, 12	66–68	_____ /2
Locating Detail on a Map	8, 20	68–76	_____ /2
Direction and Distance	14, 19	70–71	_____ /2
Using a Map Key	13, 15, 16, 17	72–74	_____ /4

Your score: _____ out of 20

Passing score: 15 out of 20

CHAPTER 3

PATTERNS IN SOCIAL STUDIES READING

"Faye, here's the basic cake recipe you wanted. First, cream the butter, then add the sugar to the butter and mix well. After that, break two eggs and add them to the mixture. Set aside the mixture. Now sift 2 cups flour with ½ teaspoon baking powder and 1 teaspoon salt. Mix the wet ingredients and the dry ingredients and pour the batter into a baking pan. Finally, bake in a 325-degree oven for 45 minutes."

"Why do I need the baking powder, Peg?"

"You need the baking powder to make the cake rise. If you tried to make a cake without baking powder, it would be flat and heavy. Baking powder makes a cake light and fluffy."

Peg just showed you some of the ways social studies material is organized. First, when she gave Faye the recipe, she emphasized the **sequence**, or order, of the steps. Then she explained the **effect** of adding the baking powder. Finally, she **compared** and **contrasted** a cake made with baking powder with one made without. In this chapter, we will be looking at these skills:

Sequence—getting things in the right order (for example, steps in a recipe)

Cause and Effect—understanding what happened and why it happened (for example, the effect of adding ingredients to a recipe)

Compare and Contrast—looking at how things and events are the same and how they are different (for example, a cake made with baking powder and a cake made without baking powder)

SEQUENCE

USING A TIMELINE

In this section you will study sequence, the organization of events in time order. Most passages present information in time order. In order to make time sequence clear, you can place events on a timeline. In this book, you will be using timelines that look like this:

The following example shows how to use this kind of timeline.

> The nineteenth century was America's Age of Invention. People like Samuel Morse, Alexander Graham Bell, and Thomas Edison developed devices that changed people's daily lives.
>
> "What hath God wrought?" were the immortal words tapped out by Samuel Morse on his telegraph key in 1837.
>
> "Mr. Watson, come here; I want you," was the first sentence ever spoken on a telephone by its inventor, Alexander Graham Bell, in 1876.
>
> "Mary had a little lamb," were the somewhat less than immortal words recorded by Thomas Edison on his gramophone in 1887.

List the events in the passage you just read on this timeline.

The three events described in the passage are the invention of the telegraph in 1837, the invention of the telephone in 1876, and the invention of the gramophone in 1887.

Your completed timeline should look like this:

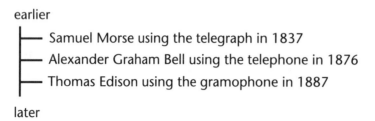

earlier
├── Samuel Morse using the telegraph in 1837
├── Alexander Graham Bell using the telephone in 1876
├── Thomas Edison using the gramophone in 1887
later

Sequence Tip
In addition to dates, words identify sequence. When putting events in time order, look for words like *soon, before, after, later, then,* and *while.*

EXERCISE 1: PUTTING EVENTS IN SEQUENCE

Passage 1
Directions: Read the following passage. Number the events listed at the end of the passage in the correct time order and then write them on the timeline below.

On January 24, 1848, while building a sawmill for John Sutter, James Marshall found some small stones that he thought might contain gold. About a week later, he went to see Sutter at the local fort to show him the stones. Sutter and Marshall tested the stones and found that they were pure gold. Despite their desire to keep their discovery quiet, word spread fast. Soon groups of men were appearing at the mill, looking for gold. Trying to get rid of them, Marshall then sent them off in all directions. To his surprise, many of them found gold. The California Gold Rush had begun.

_____ Marshall sends gold seekers off to look for gold.

_____ Marshall and Sutter test the stones to see if they are gold.

_____ Groups of men discover gold in the places where Marshall sent them.

_____ Marshall discovers gold at Sutter's mill.

earlier
├──
├──
├──
├──
later

Passage 2

Directions: Read the following passage. Make a list of the events in the passage. Then construct a timeline like the ones you have been using and put your list of events on it. You should list at least three events on your timeline.

On October 8, 1871, a cow kicked over a kerosene lamp and started the great Chicago Fire. In a few hours, the fire spread through the West Side and then jumped the South Branch of the Chicago River. The city was in flames.

Twenty-seven hours after it started, the fire was finally put out. Food, clothing, and money began pouring in from all over the world to help the destroyed city.

Your list of events:

Your timeline:

Answers start on page 203.

SEQUENCE NOT IN TIME ORDER

Passages often present events in an order different from the order in which they occurred. In those cases, you must use clues in the passage to figure out the correct time order. Often you can use dates to help you put events in order, as in the following passage.

Representing the American colonists, Thomas Jefferson read the Declaration of Independence in Philadelphia on July 4, 1776. The colonists wanted independence from Great Britain because of many conflicts with England.

For example, in 1763, the British had decided that no colonists would be allowed to settle west of the Allegheny Mountains. This angered many colonists who had hoped to move west. Then the Sugar Act of 1764 and the Stamp Act of 1765 forced the colonists to pay heavy taxes to England. Colonists throughout the thirteen colonies opposed these actions. Ten years later, in 1775, the opposition had grown so strong that fighting broke out between the British and the colonists of Massachusetts. It was only a matter of time before the colonies would become an independent nation.

Number the following events in correct time order, using clues from the passage.

_____ Thomas Jefferson reads the Declaration of Independence.

_____ British ban the colonists from moving west of the Allegheny Mountains.

_____ Fighting breaks out between the British and the colonists of Massachusetts.

_____ The British force the colonists to pay heavy taxes.

Now place the events in order on the timeline below.

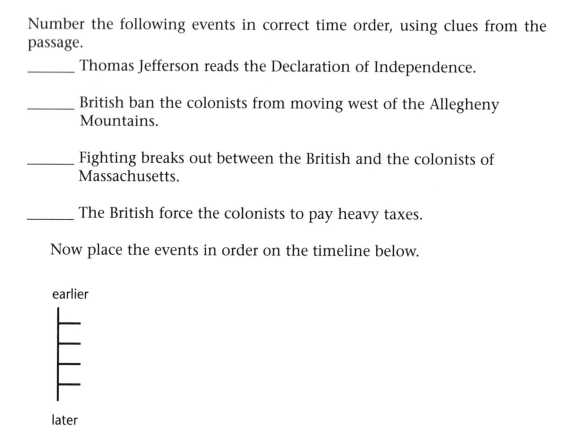

In this passage, the writer presents events out of time order in order to emphasize the main point. The main idea, that the Declaration of Independence was the result of a long series of conflicts, is made in the first sentence. The description of events in the second paragraph supports that main idea. Even though the reading of the Declaration of Independence happened after the other events, the author mentions it first in order to make his main idea clear. Your completed timeline should look like this:

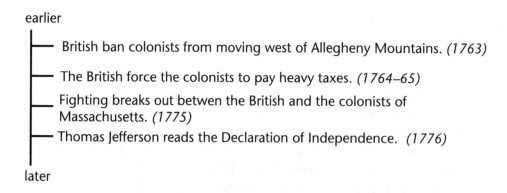

EXERCISE 2: USING DATES TO IDENTIFY SEQUENCE

Directions: Following the passage on page 91 is a list of the events described in the passage. Number the events, fill in their dates, and place them in correct order on the timeline.

Following the European discovery of America by Christopher Columbus in 1492, other nations sent explorers and settlers to North America. The Spanish were ruthless and bloodthirsty. One Spanish explorer, Hernando De Soto, marched through the southeastern United States from 1539 to 1542. He used torture to force the Native Americans to lead him to gold. Since there was almost no gold to be found, he killed many Native Americans. The worst massacre occurred at their settlement at Mabila on the Alabama River, where De Soto's men murdered several thousand Native Americans.

The French also sent explorers to North America, but they treated the Native Americans well and traded with them. When Jacques Cartier discovered the mouth of the St. Lawrence River in 1534, he opened up Canada to French exploration. From 1603 to 1615, Samuel de Champlain explored parts of southern Canada and northern New York and established the fur trade with the Native Americans. Over fifty years later, Marquette and Joliet traveled down the Mississippi River as far as Arkansas, establishing French claims to the entire Mississippi valley.

_____ Columbus discovers America.

date: _____

_____ De Soto murders thousands of Native Americans at Mabila.

approximate date: _____

_____ Cartier discovers the mouth of the St. Lawrence River.

date: _____

_____ Marquette and Joliet travel down the Mississippi River.

approximate date: _____

_____ Champlain establishes the fur trade with the Native Americans.

approximate date: _____

earlier

later

Answers start on page 203.

SEQUENCE IN GRAPHS

A line graph is well suited to showing a trend over time. By showing how something changes over time, a graph illustrates a sequence very clearly. The following line graph traces the price of chicken at Piggle-Wiggle Supermarkets from 1988 to 1995. Answer the question following the graph by circling the correct choice.

PRICE OF CHICKEN AT PIGGLE-WIGGLE MARKETS

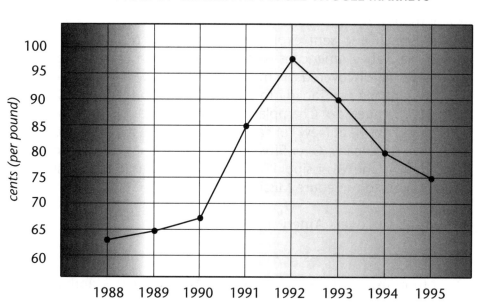

Between 1988 and 1992, the price of chicken at Piggle-Wiggle Markets

(1) went down
(2) went up
(3) went down and then up
(4) went up and then down
(5) remained steady

You were correct if you circled choice (2). Find the data points for 1988 and 1992. Now look at the part of the line between them. The line goes up at each point. This means that the price of chicken went up from 1988 to 1992.

EXERCISE 3: SEQUENCE IN GRAPHS

Directions: Study the following graph, then choose the number of the correct answer to each question.

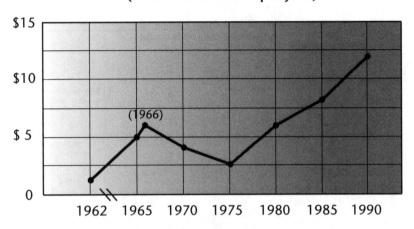

HOW MUCH NASA SPENT
(in billions of dollars per year)

Source: U.S. National Aeronautics and Space Administration

1. Between 1965 and 1970, NASA spending

   (1) rose and then fell
   (2) dropped steadily
   (3) rose slightly
   (4) remained constant
   (5) dropped and then rose

2. Between 1980 and 1990, NASA spending

   (1) decreased
   (2) increased
   (3) increased then decreased
   (4) decreased then increased
   (5) remained level

3. Which of the following best describes the pattern of NASA spending between 1962 and 1990?

   (1) It rose steadily.
   (2) It rose, then fell.
   (3) It peaked in 1975.
   (4) It rose until 1966, fell until 1980, then rose again.
   (5) It rose until 1966, fell until 1975, then rose again.

Answers start on page 203.

SEQUENCE ON EXPEDITION MAPS

Maps can depict a chain of events or changes over time. For example, the route of an explorer or an army could be traced on a map. Study the following example to see how looking at the route of the explorers Lewis and Clark can help us understand their journey.

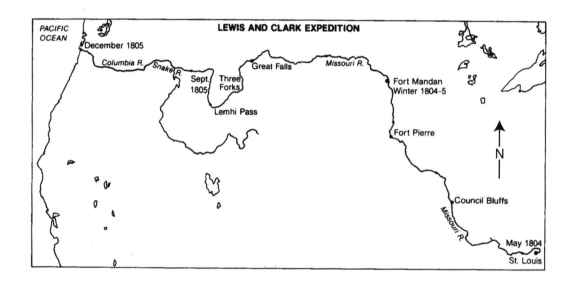

▶ When did Lewis and Clark leave St. Louis? _____

In order to find when Lewis and Clark left St. Louis, you must find St. Louis on the map. If you are not sure where St. Louis is, trace along the line that represents the route of Lewis and Clark until you find St. Louis. It is at the eastern end of their route. The date May 1804 is written next to the city. That is the date that Lewis and Clark left St. Louis.

▶ Where did Lewis and Clark spend the winter of 1804–5? _____

_____

Trace the route of the expedition until you find Winter 1804–5. Winter 1804–5 is written below Fort Mandan. Therefore, they spent the winter at Fort Mandan.

▶ When did Lewis and Clark reach the Pacific Ocean? _____

Trace the route of the expedition until it reaches the Pacific Ocean. You should find the date December 1805, which is the date the expedition reached the Pacific Ocean.

EXERCISE 4: EXPEDITION MAPS

Directions: Answer each question by circling the number of the correct choice. This map shows the route of a famous explorer through what is now the southeastern United States.

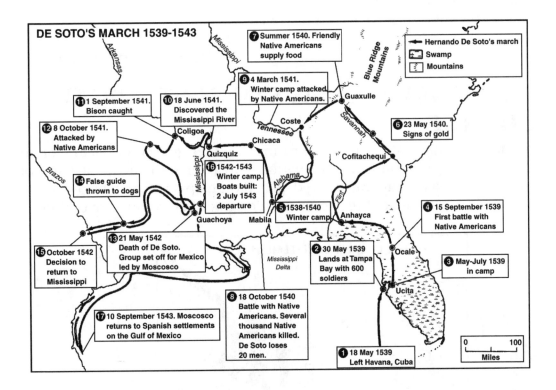

1. Where did De Soto first enter what is now the United States?

   (1) Havana, Cuba
   (2) Mississippi Delta
   (3) Brazos River
   (4) Tampa Bay
   (5) Guachoya

2. Where did friendly Native Americans supply food to De Soto?

   (1) Tampa Bay
   (2) Quizquiz
   (3) Guaxulle
   (4) Mabila
   (5) Ocale

3. When did De Soto die?

   (1) September 1539
   (2) October 1540
   (3) June 1541
   (4) May 1542
   (5) September 1543

4. What important event happened at Quizquiz?

(1) Several thousand Native Americans were killed.
(2) De Soto died.
(3) Friendly Native Americans supplied food.
(4) A bison was caught.
(5) The Mississippi River was discovered.

Answers start on page 203.

SEQUENCE ON MAPS OF HISTORICAL CHANGE

Maps can illustrate a trend over time of either growth or decline of an area. The varying boundaries of nations, areas of settlement, or areas of production of a product can all be depicted on maps. The map below shows the pattern of settlement of the thirteen original U.S. colonies over time.

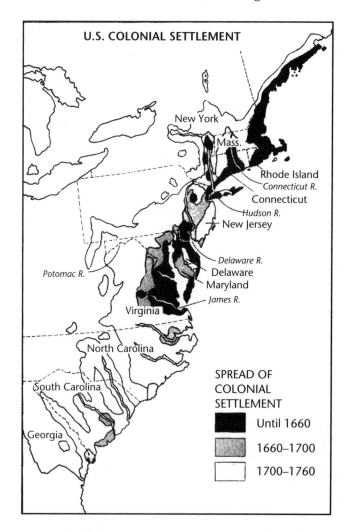

▶ Until 1660, most of the settlement was along the coast of the Atlantic Ocean. True or False? _____

You were right if you thought the statement was true. Find the areas that match the key for the areas settled before 1660. These areas are mainly along the coast, as well as along the James, Hudson, and Connecticut rivers.

▶ In general, most of the early colonists settled south of Virginia, with settlement spreading north in later years. True or False? _____

You were right if you thought the statement was false. Just the opposite is true. The early settlement was in the northern part of the country from Maine to Virginia. Settlement then spread south through the Carolinas and Georgia.

▶ With the passage of time, settlement spread inland from the coast. True or False? _____

You were right if you thought the statement was true. The area for 1660–1700 and the area for 1700–1760 show a steady growth inland.

EXERCISE 5: READING MAPS OF HISTORICAL CHANGE

Directions: Mark each statement true (T) or false (F) based on the map. This map shows how the United States expanded into its current 48 continental states.

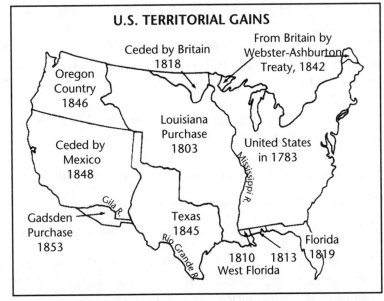

_____ 1. The Southwest was ceded by Mexico after the Oregon Country was already under United States control.

_____ 2. The Louisiana Purchase was the first major territorial gain for the United States after 1783.

_____ 3. After the Mexican cession in 1848, the United States controlled all the land that would become the continental 48 states.

_____ 4. Florida was completely under the control of the United States by 1813.

Answers start on page 204.

UNDERSTANDING CAUSE AND EFFECT

IDENTIFYING CAUSE AND EFFECT

Every day you are affected by what goes on around you. In order to function in your daily life, you have to understand cause and effect. For example, if your family didn't pay the rent every month, you would be evicted from your home. The cause would be not paying the rent. The effect would be eviction.

cause: *effect*:
not paying rent ⎯⎯⎯⟶ eviction

Sometimes cause and effect can be very clear. A sixteen-year-old student cuts school sixty-eight days. The effect is that she is not promoted. At other times, cause-and-effect relationships are less clear. "I wish I knew what I could have done to help him stop drinking." Much of political debate is about causes and effects. One politician says, "If we raise taxes, the economy will improve." At the same time, another says, "If we lower taxes, the economy will improve."

When reading social studies passages, you should ask yourself, "What happened?" and "Why did it happen?" When you answer the question "What happened?" you understand the *effect*. When you answer the question "Why did it happen?" you understand the *cause*. Your reading will often contain clues that can help you decide what is the cause and what is the effect.

Read the following sentence. Decide what happened and why it happened, and fill in the blanks.

Because it was mismanaged, the company went bankrupt.

▶ What happened? _____

▶ Why did it happen? _____

You should have written "The company went bankrupt" as the answer to the first question and "Because it was mismanaged" as the answer to the second. *Because* is a clue word for the *cause* or the answer to "Why did it happen?"

Cause and Effect Tip

Watch for cause-and-effect clue words and phrases in your reading like *because* and *as a result of. Before* and *after* sometimes also function as cause-and-effect clue words.

EXERCISE 6: IDENTIFYING CAUSE AND EFFECT

Directions: For each sentence, decide what happened (the effect) and why it happened (the cause) and then fill in the blanks with your choices.

1. Because the wholesale price of coffee had dropped 25%, Colombia found itself in financial trouble.

   What happened? _____

   Why did it happen? _____

2. The American West developed rapidly after the Civil War because of the railroads.

   What happened? _____

   Why did it happen? _____

3. Oil prices increased dramatically as a result of the formation of the oil cartel OPEC in 1973.

   What happened? _____

   Why did it happen? _____

4. After man-made (synthetic) rubber was developed, the price of natural rubber dropped.

   What happened? _____

   Why did it happen? _____

Answers start on page 204.

IDENTIFYING CAUSE AND EFFECT IN A PASSAGE

You cannot depend on a cause and effect always being in the same sentence or being clearly pointed out. You should remember to ask the key questions: "What happened?" (effect) and "Why did it happen?" (cause). In the paragraph below, underline the cause and circle the effect.

> Mothers Against Drunk Drivers (MADD), Students Against Drunk Drivers (SADD), and Bartenders Against Drunk Drivers (BADD) have all campaigned against driving while drinking. The result has been a decrease in traffic accidents.

The key word *result* can help you find what happened (the effect): a decrease in traffic accidents. The first sentence explains why it happened (the cause): MADD, SADD, and BADD all campaigned against drunk driving.

EXERCISE 7: CAUSE AND EFFECT IN A PASSAGE

Directions: Following each passage are questions about cause and effect. Circle the number of the correct choice.

> Our continent is named for one of the greatest frauds of all time, Amerigo Vespucci. Vespucci helped outfit Columbus's fleet for his third voyage in 1498. During that voyage, Columbus first sighted the mainland of America. In order to beat Columbus's claim, Vespucci published an account of a voyage he had headed in 1497. This voyage never took place.
>
> After reading Vespucci's false account, the king of Portugal asked him to accompany the Portuguese explorer Coelho and write about the voyage. Vespucci went on two voyages commanded by Coelho. In his writings, he took full credit for both voyages and never mentioned Coelho.
>
> Vespucci's accounts were read by many people because he included stories of native sexual customs. In 1507, a young professor of geography in France placed the name *America* on what we now call *South America*. The name caught on. By the time people agreed that Columbus had really discovered the New World, it was too late. The name *America* had been given to the entire New World.

1. What was the effect of Vespucci's false account of his voyage to the new world in 1497?

   (1) Vespucci became the first explorer to discover America.
   (2) The King of Portugal forced Vespucci to leave Portugal.
   (3) The King of Portugal asked Vespucci to accompany Coelho.
   (4) Coelho gave Vespucci credit for Coelho's expeditions.
   (5) Coelho came to value Vespucci's great knowledge of America.

2. What caused Vespucci's accounts of his voyages with Coelho to be read by so many people?

   (1) He wrote about native sexual customs.
   (2) Vespucci made Coelho famous.
   (3) The whole world focused on the daring Portuguese explorers.
   (4) A French geography professor had all his students study Vespucci's work.
   (5) Vespucci was the famous discoverer of America.

> Less oil is being spilled into American waters these days—83% less than in 1984. That's because petroleum companies have been taking greater care to avoid accidents since the wreck of the *Exxon Valdez* demonstrated how expensive a major oil spill can be. Exxon claims to have already spent almost $7 billion to clean

up the spill and compensate victims. The company will be forced to pay even more when pending lawsuits are decided. Other oil companies have taken notice, so they've adopted new safety procedures and bought new cleanup equipment to make sure they never have to pay such high damages.

3. There are fewer oil spills in U.S. waters because

    (1) oil companies are going out of business
    (2) Americans are using less oil
    (3) oil is produced in other countries
    (4) Exxon pays to clean up oil spills
    (5) oil companies are being careful to avoid spills

4. Oil companies have bought new cleanup equipment because

    (1) the equipment is required by new laws
    (2) the public has put pressure on the oil companies
    (3) the equipment is less expensive than it used to be
    (4) the companies want to avoid expensive lawsuits
    (5) the old equipment was used to clean up the *Valdez* spill

In the 1920s, psychologists Hugh Hartshorne and Mark A. May studied the development of honesty by testing 11,000 children. As a result of the tests, they decided that the children did not develop honesty as a result of preaching by adults. Instead, they learned honesty mainly through personal relationships and social situations.

Hartshorne and May saw the children imitating adult and peer models a great deal. In other words, they found that the children did what they saw others do, not what they were told to do. If the children were surrounded by lying, cheating, and stealing, they tended to lie, cheat, and steal. If the people they imitated were honest, they tended to be honest.

5. According to Hartshorne and May, children are likely to be honest if

    (1) they are often in social situations
    (2) the people around them are honest
    (3) they are told they should be honest
    (4) their families have plenty of money
    (5) they are punished for dishonesty

Answers start on page 204.

APPLYING CAUSE AND EFFECT

Government has a strong effect on our lives as Americans. American blacks are one group whose lives have been affected, for good or bad, by the actions of the government. In the next exercise, you will be asked to match four actions of government with the effect each action might have had on an individual person.

EXERCISE 8: APPLYING CAUSE AND EFFECT

Directions: Below are listed four documents that greatly influenced conditions for black Americans. Below the documents are quotes that describe the effect of each of these documents. Match each government action with the quote it made possible.

a. Emancipation Proclamation—1863
    President Lincoln ordered an end to slavery in the Confederate states.

b. Supreme Court separate-but-equal decision—1896
    Segregation of public facilities such as schools was declared legal
    by the Supreme Court.

c. Voting Rights Act—1965
    Laws preventing black people from voting were banned by Congress.

d. Civil Rights Act—1964
    Discrimination in public places was banned by Congress.

_____ 1. "As our first black mayor, I pledge to serve all the people."

_____ 2. "I remember when I had to sit in the back of the bus. Now I can
             sit where I please."

_____ 3. "I have to go to a separate school from white people. Some
             people say it is just as good, but I don't believe them."

_____ 4. "I'm a free man now. I'm going to join the Union army and
             fight the slaveholders."

Answers start on page 204.

COMPARISON AND CONTRAST
LOOKING AT SIMILARITIES

> Despite the great differences among human societies, anthropologists have found an institution they all share. All societies have some form of marriage.

The above paragraph compares the societies of the world. It looks for similarities shared by all and finds one: marriage. A **comparison** can show how two or more things are alike. Read the following paragraph. Then, in the blank provided, write one way that the Coney Island amusement parks were similar.

> New York's Coney Island amusement parks were all designed to send people into a world of pleasure. For instance, Steeplechase Park was nicknamed "The Funny Place." It featured rides such as the human roulette wheel, which sent riders whirling and sprawling. Its "Blowhole Theatre" contained hidden air jets that blew off men's hats and sent ladies' skirts flying up around their waists. Luna Park was a dream city of bright colors and fanciful decorations. It was exotic, rich, and magical. Visitors felt as though they had entered a foreign land when they walked through the gates of Luna Park.

▶ How were all the amusement parks similar?

_____

The first sentence tells you that all the parks were designed to send people into a world of pleasure. The clue word *all* tells you that a similarity is being described.

EXERCISE 9: IDENTIFYING SIMILARITIES

Directions: In your own words, answer the questions following each passage.

The populations of three major races, the Caucasians, the Negroes, and the Mongolians, all developed in a similar way. Large numbers of each race abandoned hunting and gathering and turned to agriculture. The result in each case was population growth among the agricultural groups. Those groups that remained hunters and gatherers, such as the Pygmies and Bushmen of Africa and the aborigines of Australia, now make up only a tiny percentage of the world population.

1. Why did the three major races all experience population growth?

   _____

2. How are the Pygmies and Bushmen of Africa and the aborigines of Australia similar?

   _____

The two nations of Great Britain and Japan have much in common. Both are large island nations separated from the mainland by narrow bodies of water. Both were once major military powers controlling vast amounts of land and millions of people. While neither is important today for its military might, both Great Britain and Japan are important industrial and trading nations.

3. How is the geography of Great Britain and Japan similar?

   _____

4. How is the history of Japan and Great Britain similar?

   _____

5. How are the economies of Great Britain and Japan similar today?

   _____

Possible answers start on page 204.

LOOKING AT DIFFERENCES

You have looked at similarities. Now you will look at differences. When you **contrast** two things, you concentrate on how they are different. Examining differences as well as similarities helps you get a better picture of what you are studying. Read the following example passage, then use the information in the passage to fill in the chart.

In the past 200 years, technology has changed our lives radically. For example, while our ancestors depended on horses to travel long distances, today we travel from coast to coast in a few hours on an airplane. When we want to get around town, we may drive a car, or we may take a high-speed subway train.

Another dramatic change we have experienced has been in communication. The Battle of New Orleans was fought because neither side knew that the War of 1812 had already ended. It took weeks for the news to travel by boat from England to the United States. Today, through radio and television, we have almost instant access to world events. In addition, world leaders can talk on the telephone even though they may be separated by an ocean.

Now use the information in the passage above to fill in the chart below. In your own words, write information in each box that contrasts travel and communication today and 200 years ago.

CONTRAST: 200 YEARS AGO AND TODAY		
	200 Years Ago	**Today**
travel		
overseas communication		

Your chart might look something like this. Did you show how different things are now than they were 200 years ago?

CONTRAST: 200 YEARS AGO AND TODAY		
	200 Years Ago	**Today**
travel	depended on horses, so long-distance travel very slow	can get around town or even coast to coast very fast
overseas communication	messages had to travel by boat across the ocean	now can talk on the phone overseas; hear radio and TV news the same day something happens

EXERCISE 10: IDENTIFYING CONTRASTS

Directions: Read the following passage. Then fill in the chart to show how the Uptown Jews and the Downtown Jews were different.

By the late 1800s, New York City was home for two very different groups of Jewish people: the Uptown Jews and the Downtown Jews. The Uptown Jews were of German descent, but they had been born in America. They settled in the wealthy Upper East Side and Upper West Side neighborhoods of New York City. They were Reform Jews, so they did not *keep kosher* (follow Jewish dietary laws).

These Uptown Jews differed in many ways from the Jews who were joining them in New York City. The Downtown Jews came to this country from Eastern Europe in the late 1800s. Most of them had very little money. They moved into the poorer Lower East Side neighborhoods. As Orthodox Jews, they followed more traditional Jewish practices than the Uptown Jews and continued to keep kosher.

	Uptown Jews	Downtown Jews
Where were they born?		
Where did they live in New York City?		
Did they keep kosher?		
Were they wealthy?		

Answers start on page 205.

COMPARISON AND CONTRAST IN ILLUSTRATIONS

Maps, charts, and graphs can be used to illustrate comparison and contrast. For example, the map on page 107 compares and contrasts black voting rights in Southern states during the early years of the civil rights movement. Answer the questions based on the map.

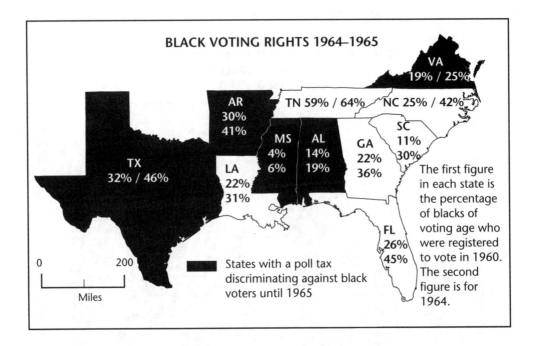

BLACK VOTING RIGHTS 1964–1965

VA 19% / 25%

AR 30% 41%

TN 59% / 64%   NC 25% / 42%

SC 11% 30%

MS 4% 6%   AL 14% 19%   GA 22% 36%

TX 32% / 46%

LA 22% 31%

FL 26% 45%

The first figure in each state is the percentage of blacks of voting age who were registered to vote in 1960. The second figure is for 1964.

0   200

Miles

States with a poll tax discriminating against black voters until 1965

▶ Which five states used a poll tax to discriminate against blacks until 1965? _____

You were right if you listed Texas, Arkansas, Mississippi, Alabama, and Virginia. These states are all shaded black on the map, showing that they used a poll tax.

▶ Between 1960 and 1964, did North Carolina or South Carolina have a greater increase in the percentage of registered black voters?

_____

You were right if you said South Carolina had a greater increase, from 11% to 30%, or an increase of 19%. North Carolina increased from 25% to 42%, or an increase of 17%.

EXERCISE 11: COMPARISON AND CONTRAST IN ILLUSTRATIONS

Directions: Mark each statement *T* if it is true or *F* if it is false.

Questions 1–2 are based on the map "Black Voting Rights" above.

_____ 1. Of all the states shown, Mississippi showed the smallest increase in black voter registration—only 2% between 1960 and 1964.

_____ 2. In 1964, Texas had the highest percentage of any southern state of eligible blacks registered, with 46%.

Questions 3–6 are based on the following line graph.

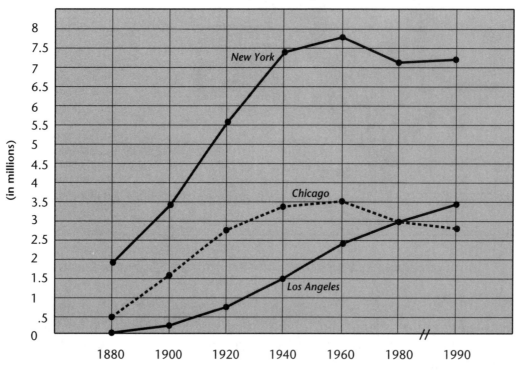

**THE THREE LARGEST CITIES IN 1990 AND THEIR
POPULATIONS IN EARLIER YEARS
(1880–1990)**

Source: U.S. Bureau of the Census

_____ 3. When the population of New York City was increasing, the population of Chicago was also increasing.

_____ 4. New York and Chicago have always had about the same population.

_____ 5. In 1980, Chicago and Los Angeles had about the same population.

_____ 6. When the population of Chicago was decreasing, the population of Los Angeles was also decreasing.

Answers start on page 205.

EXERCISE 12: CHAPTER REVIEW

Directions: Study each passage or illustration carefully. Then choose the correct answer to each question.

Questions 1–3 are based on the following map.

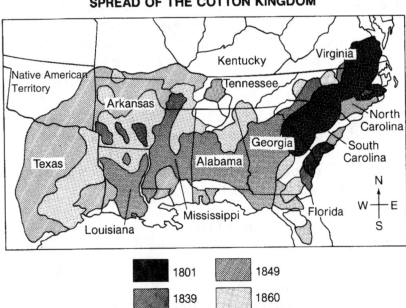

SPREAD OF THE COTTON KINGDOM

1. In 1801, the Cotton Kingdom was centered in

    (1) Texas, Native American Territory, and Arkansas
    (2) the Carolinas, Georgia, and Virginia
    (3) Georgia, Alabama, Mississippi, and Louisiana
    (4) Florida and Texas
    (5) Tennessee, Alabama, and Mississippi

2. From 1801 to 1860, the spread of the Cotton Kingdom was to

    (1) the north and east
    (2) the south and west
    (3) the east
    (4) Illinois
    (5) the Atlantic coast

3. The areas that had the greatest growth from 1801 to 1839 in land devoted to cotton were

    (1) Texas, Native American Territory, and Arkansas
    (2) the Carolinas, Georgia, and Virginia
    (3) Georgia, Alabama, Mississippi, and Louisiana
    (4) Florida and Texas
    (5) Tennessee, Kentucky, and North Carolina

Questions 4–5 are based on the following passage.

The epidemic of adolescent drug abuse continues to rage across the nation. Many reasons are given to explain this problem. Some people say that parents are too easy on their children. Other people say that the problem is caused by people drifting away from religion. Probably one of the main causes of the problem is peer pressure—teenagers just want to be part of the gang. Another reason kids take drugs is the desire to escape reality. Drugs seem to provide a way out from the pressures of growing up. Drugs also seem glamorous because they are forbidden.

The effects of drug abuse can be devastating. A drug abuser might radically change in both appearance and behavior. The desperate need for money to buy drugs can lead the user to prostitution or robbery. In addition, adolescent drug abuse places a terrible strain on family relationships.

4. According to the passage, one of the main causes of adolescent drug abuse is probably

(1) peer pressure
(2) strained family relationships
(3) a radical change in appearance and behavior
(4) a desperate need for money
(5) teen prostitution

5. According to the passage, drug abuse may cause an adolescent to

(1) drift away from religion
(2) commit crimes
(3) want to be part of the gang
(4) become more loving toward his or her family
(5) improve his or her appearance

Questions 6–10 are based on the following passage.

When high-tech industries are struggling, the next high-tech boom may be getting started. When laid-off executives and scientists don't have enough to do, they dream of running their own companies or building new products. So they start new companies offering new products.

Thus, while the giant companies suffer through hard times, dozens of new companies are quietly setting up shop. Often these new firms create the new products of the next boom. When these breakthrough products capture the public's imagination, the new boom explodes. Old and new firms rush to copy the product. The industry shoots into a period of frantic growth that may last two years or more.

Then the public's love affair with the product ends. Or a giant company takes over the whole market. Then the boom is over. The industry slumps back into the next recession. This bust-boom-bust cycle has happened over and over in high technology: in the late 1960s with minicomputers, in the mid-'70s with video games, in the early '80s with personal computers and VCRs, and in the early '90s with video camcorders and cellular phones.

6. How were the high-tech booms of the late 1960s, the mid-'70s, the early '80s, and the early '90s similar?

   (1) They all got started when new firms introduced new products.
   (2) They were all related to the car industry.
   (3) They all ended when one giant company took over the market.
   (4) They all began during times of prosperity.
   (5) They were all dominated by the Japanese.

7. How were the high-tech booms of the late 1960s, the mid-'70s, the early '80s, and the early '90s different?

   (1) Their patterns of boom and decline are different.
   (2) Only in the mid-'70s did firms rush to copy the new product.
   (3) Only in the early '80s was there a major new breakthrough product.
   (4) Different products led each boom.
   (5) Economic conditions were very different while the new products and new companies were getting started.

8. What is the correct sequence of each high-tech boom cycle?

   (1) large companies develop new product, new market booms, industry slumps
   (2) development during previous boom, short recession, new boom
   (3) development of new product by new firm during slow period, boom, industry slump
   (4) company mergers, development of new product, booming new market, leveling off
   (5) mass advertising campaign, booming sales, new firms created, period of stability

9. What is one of the causes of a high-tech boom?

   (1) planning by giant corporations during times of prosperity
   (2) government regulation that directs the industry in the most productive direction
   (3) executives and scientists developing firms and products during a slow period
   (4) a giant competitor dominating the market
   (5) market surveys that indicate the area of greatest consumer need

10. According to the passage, which of the following might cause a high-tech boom to end?

(1) scientists developing a new product
(2) the public losing interest in the new product
(3) other firms copying the product
(4) computers becoming obsolete
(5) executives getting laid off

Answers start on page 205.

CHAPTER REVIEW EVALUATION CHART			
Skill	**Question Numbers***	**Review Pages**	**Number Correct**
Sequence	**1, 2, 3**, 8	86–97	_____ /4
Cause-Effect	4, 5, 9,10	98–102	_____ /4
Compare-Contrast	6, 7	103–108	_____ /2

*Question numbers in **dark type** are based on illustrations.

Your score: _____ out of 10

Passing score: 7 out of 10

CHAPTER 4

ANALYZING SOCIAL STUDIES PASSAGES

Eileen's eighteen-year-old son Greg just got his driver's license. As Eileen walked into the house with two bags of groceries, Greg rushed to her side, took the bags from her, and put away the groceries. When he finished, Eileen said, "OK, you can have the car tonight."

Eileen was using her analytical skills. She looked at the facts: Greg had never helped her with the groceries before. Greg had just gotten his driver's license.

She realized that he must be helping her in order to get something else. He must want to use the car. Greg also was using his analytical skills. He predicted that if he helped his mother she might let him use her car.

In this chapter, you will be practicing these analytical skills:

1. Distinguishing fact from opinion

   fact: Greg is helping with the groceries.
   opinion: Greg is a good son.

2. Making inferences, or reading between the lines

   Greg helps me only when he wants something. He is helping me now. Therefore, he must want something.

3. Developing a hypothesis, or educated guess

Since Greg just got his license, a reasonable explanation of why he is helping is that he wants to use the car.

4. Predicting an outcome

Mom will let me use the car if I help her with the groceries.

You will also begin to study political cartoons and how they use comedy and exaggeration to express opinions.

FACT AND OPINION

DISTINGUISHING FACT FROM OPINION

A *fact* is a statement that can be proven. An *opinion* is a belief that cannot be proven. If someone believes that something is true, it still has to be proven to be a fact. Every day, you read and hear both facts and opinions. At times, you may have to give some thought to which is which. When you read social studies material, take note of whether a statement you read is fact or opinion. Can a statement be proven? Or is it something the author believes but cannot prove?

Of the following two statements, one is a fact and one is an opinion. Write *F* in the blank before the fact and *O* in the blank before the opinion.

_____   The U.S. Constitution is the greatest political document
            ever written.

_____   In 1985, there were twenty-six amendments to the U.S.
            Constitution.

You were right if you thought the first statement was an opinion. The word *greatest* gives the opinion of the writer. The second statement is a fact that can be checked by looking at a copy of the Constitution.

EXERCISE 1: FACT OR OPINION?

Directions: In the blank preceding each sentence, write *F* if the sentence is a fact and *O* if it is an opinion.

1. _____   The United States is a democracy in which people elect
               their government officials.

2. _____   Democracy is the best form of government.

3. _____ Local governments mismanage their responsibilities of police and fire protection.

4. _____ Local governments have responsibility for the public schools.

5. _____ All citizens over the age of eighteen have the right to register and vote.

6 _____ The vice president has the most unimportant job in the entire federal government.

7. _____ If the president dies in office, the vice president becomes the new president.

Answers start on page 205.

FACTS AND OPINIONS IN A PASSAGE

Writers often tell you facts and express their opinions in the same piece of writing. They use the facts as evidence to back up their opinions. In the following example, see how the author uses facts to support her opinion. Read the paragraph and underline the sentences that contain facts. Circle the sentences that contain opinions.

> The United States is a member of the North Atlantic Treaty Organization (NATO). The members of NATO coordinate their military activity in Europe through the NATO military command. Because we have to work through the NATO chain of command, NATO restricts our ability to act on our own. We should withdraw from NATO because our military needs to be able to work freely in Europe.

The first two sentences are facts. The writer can prove that the United States is a member of NATO. She can also prove that NATO has a military command that coordinates the activity of member nations in Europe. The second two sentences are opinions. It is her opinion that membership in NATO restricts our ability to act on our own. In the last sentence, the word *should* is a clue that the sentence is the opinion of the author. She is telling you what she thinks *should* happen.

Fact vs. Opinion Tip

Phrases like *I think*, *I believe*, and *we should* tell you that the writer is expressing an opinion.

EXERCISE 2: FACTS AND OPINIONS IN A PASSAGE

Directions: For each sentence in each of the following passages, write *F* if the sentence is a fact and *O* if the sentence is an opinion.

Passage 1

(a) The best political system ever developed is the two-party system of the United States. (b) Since the Civil War, no third party has been able to threaten the political power of either the Democratic Party or the Republican Party. (c) Every president of the last one hundred years has been a member of one of these two parties. (d) No third party has been able to gain control of either house of Congress. (e) The country has been spared the chaos that results when there are more than two parties. (f) And the people have not had to endure the tyranny of one-party rule.

a. _____   d. _____

b. _____   e. _____

c. _____   f. _____

Passage 2

(a) The book *The Hard Times of Mortimer Mitchell* should not be on the shelves of our high school library. (b) First, the characters take drugs. (c) Second, there are three scenes in the book in which sexual activity between unmarried people is described in detail. (d) Third, the main character murders another character and then goes unpunished. (e) This is not the kind of book that the children in our community should read. (f) A parent committee should be formed to help the school librarian choose good reading material for our teens.

a. _____   d. _____

b. _____   e. _____

c. _____   f. _____

Answers start on page 205.

The *kibbutz* is a type of cooperative community found in Israel. In a kibbutz, most things are owned by everyone as a group. The kibbutz owns the land, all farm animals and equipment, and all crops. Sometimes it owns its own factories. In some kibbutzim, even the houses are owned by the community.

People who are willing to give all they own to the kibbutz can be considered for membership. However, in certain kibbutzim, incoming members must also be under thirty-five years old. Older people are not allowed to join unless they marry a kibbutz member or their child is a kibbutz member. This ban came as a result of hard experience. Many older people were set in their ways and unable to adjust to the needs of the kibbutz. After a very unpleasant period, they would drop out of the kibbutz, leaving anger and bitterness on both sides.

4. A kibbutz is a community in which

   (1) everybody must learn Hebrew, the language of Israel
   (2) new members must be over thirty-five years old
   (3) most things are owned in common
   (4) children cannot live with their parents
   (5) factories are owned by the richest people

5. A good reason for not allowing new members over thirty-five is

   (1) they have trouble adjusting to the kibbutz way of life
   (2) they will take advantage of the younger people
   (3) they cannot work as hard as younger people
   (4) they cannot give enough money to the kibbutz
   (5) they will try to take over the kibbutz and change all the rules

Answers start on page 208.

ERRORS IN REASONING

In this chapter, you have already seen two sources of mistakes in reasoning: not having enough information and having the wrong kind of information. In this section, you will practice recognizing other errors in reasoning, such as

(a) substituting personal beliefs, desires, or experience for facts:

"I have never gotten a parking ticket on this street; therefore, it must be legal to park here."

(b) making general statements based on one example:

"All those TV offers are rip-offs. My sister sent in $25 for a set of knives, and she never got it."

(c) backward reasoning:

"If all American voters are people over eighteen years old, then all people over eighteen years old are American voters."

Below are two reasons for a certain action. Put a check (✔) in front of the one that shows good reasoning. Put an X in front of the one that shows a reasoning error.

Cali, the office manager, is trying to decide whether to purchase new word processing equipment for her office.

_____   The staff will get more work done if word processing equipment is purchased and used.

_____   Cali thinks the office ought to have the latest and fanciest equipment.

You should have put a check in front of the first reason. A good reason for purchasing new equipment is to improve productivity. You should have put an X in front of the second reason. This is an example of substituting a personal desire for good reasons.

EXERCISE 5: RECOGNIZING ERRORS IN REASONING

Directions: Following each statement are two reasons for making a choice or taking an action. Put a check (✔) in the blank before the choice that shows good reasoning. Put an X in the blank before the choice that shows a reasoning error.

1. Sandy is planning to send his son Gary to college.

_____ **a.** Since Sandy went to college, his son should go too.

_____ **b.** Since Gary wants to become a doctor, he has to go to college.

2. Mel's Auto Body Shop is in financial trouble.

_____ **a.** Since Mel's business has had an excellent financial record for thirty years, Mel is confident his bank will help him.

_____ **b.** Since the government bailed out the Chrysler Corporation when it was in financial trouble, it will help out Mel's Auto Body Shop.

3. The Yellowbrick neighborhood decided not to work with the Froston Redevelopment Authority to improve the neighborhood.

_____ **a.** The Froston Redevelopment Authority wiped out the West End neighborhood thirty years ago. Therefore, the same thing will happen to the Yellowbrick neighborhood.

_____ **b.** Over thirty years, the Froston Redevelopment Authority has constantly ignored the wishes of Froston's neighborhoods. Instead, it has listened to wealthy developers. Therefore, it is risky to work with them.

Answers start on page 209.

WHAT IS THE PROBLEM HERE?

It is important for you to be able to explain why reasoning is correct or why it is wrong. In the following exercise, you'll practice identifying and explaining reasoning problems. Try answering the questions based on the following cartoon.

Background clues: Compared to many diseases, AIDS is difficult to catch. Yet, because it is deadly, many people have irrational fears.

▶ Why is the person in this cartoon fired? _____

▶ Why is it ridiculous that this person is getting fired? _____

The boss is afraid Wilson might have AIDS. It is impossible for the employee to have caught AIDS through this string of people, and it's impossible for AIDS to be passed on through normal office contact.

Now try some sample questions based on the following paragraph.

A recent research study found that violent behavior might be caused by brain damage and child abuse. All the residents of death row spoken to by the researchers had some brain damage and had been abused in childhood. Because of the results of this study, we should put all brain-damaged people who have been victims of child abuse into mental hospitals.

▶ What does the author suggest should happen to people who have suffered child abuse and brain damage? _____

▶ What is the problem with his reasoning? _____

The author thinks that these people should be put into mental hospitals. His reasoning is poor because he is reasoning backward. The report stated that the violent people studied were brain-damaged and abused as children. That does not mean that all brain-damaged and abused people will be violent.

EXERCISE 6: ERRORS IN REASONING
Directions: Answer the questions following each passage.

In 1980, Ronald Reagan was running for president against President Jimmy Carter. He asked the voters if they were better off then than they were four years before. He suggested that, if they were worse off, they should vote for him to replace President Carter. I had had a hard year. My wife died, and my children dropped out of school. I started drinking and got fired from my job. I was doing much worse than four years before. Therefore, I voted for Ronald Reagan for president.

1. The writer of the passage decided to vote for Ronald Reagan because
   (1) he supported Reagan's economic policies
   (2) his life was going badly
   (3) he did not like Jimmy Carter
   (4) he felt that it was time for a change
   (5) he thought Reagan was a great speaker

2. What is the problem with his reasoning? _____

   _____

I read about a study that found that, in general, married men are the happiest group of people. Unmarried women came in second in the happiness study. They were almost as happy with their lives as married men. Unmarried men finished third in the survey. Finally, the unhappiest group in the population was married women.

I am an unmarried woman. My husband left me five years ago, and I am still miserable as a result. Therefore, the study must be wrong. The unhappiest group of people are unmarried women.

3. The study found that the unhappiest group was

    (1) married men
    (2) married women
    (3) unmarried men
    (4) unmarried women
    (5) children

4. What is the problem with the speaker's reasoning? _____

    _____

    It is the role of government to protect its citizens from physical harm. Many Americans are injured or killed each year as a result of criminal activities. Many of these injuries are a result of the nationwide activities of organized crime. A proper and reasonable response to this situation is to have the Federal Bureau of Investigation (FBI) coordinate a nationwide effort to end organized crime.

5. The suggestion to have the FBI coordinate a nationwide effort to end organized crime is

    (1) a poor suggestion since the federal government should stay out of local affairs
    (2) a good suggestion since the FBI should be allowed to do anything it wants
    (3) a good suggestion since a national government agency should fight a national crime problem
    (4) a poor suggestion since local police officers can handle the job
    (5) a poor suggestion since not enough Americans are killed or injured by organized crime for the government to get involved

Answers start on page 209.

RECOGNIZING VALUES

Everybody has values, those things that they consider important. We often think of the United States as a nation shaped by values. Many of the early settlers from Europe came to America for religious freedom. They valued their religion more than anything else. In the Declaration of Independence, Thomas Jefferson gave three values as the basis of the new nation: life, liberty, and the pursuit of happiness.

Many things you read and see express values. It is important to be able to recognize the values of the author or of the people the author writes about. Some people have values that you may think are noble, such as consideration for others or the importance of honesty. Other values can include wanting to make money, getting what you want no matter who gets hurt, concern for world peace, and patriotism. See if you can identify the values being expressed in the cartoon below.

Background clues: The National Rifle Association (NRA) opposes all gun control laws. They believe that all law-abiding Americans have the right to own and use guns.

▶ What value is being expressed by the shop owner in the cartoon?

  (1) patriotism
  (2) world peace
  (3) human rights
  (4) freedom to carry weapons
  (5) consideration for others

The correct answer is choice (4), *freedom to carry weapons*. The caption shows that he will sell dangerous ammunition that is clearly not meant to be used against deer. The cartoon does not suggest choice (1), *patriotism*. His willingness to sell something so dangerous eliminates choices (2), (3), and (5).

EXERCISE 7: RECOGNIZING VALUES

Directions: Study each passage or cartoon; then answer the questions that follow.

> Conversations about politically correct speech have been taking place at college campuses across the nation. Some school officials, alarmed by incidents of racial and sexual harassment, have adopted speech codes prohibiting hateful language in classrooms and dormitories. They hope to protect minority students from prejudice. Opponents argue that the codes restrict students' and teachers' First Amendment right to free speech. Some students have fought the controversial codes by suing their colleges, generally with success.

1. What value did colleges hope to preserve by adopting speech codes?

   (1) quiet study areas for students
   (2) fair treatment of all people
   (3) access to education for all Americans
   (4) support of the U.S. government
   (5) separation of the sexes in schools

2. What value did opponents of the codes hope to preserve?

   (1) equality among races
   (2) pursuit of money
   (3) freedom to express ideas
   (4) racial hatred
   (5) the right to sue

Background clues: Throughout history each U.S. president has developed a special relationship with the press. The cartoon below comments on the way former President Ronald Reagan seemed to view reporters. It refers to the First Amendment to the U.S. Constitution, which protects the freedom of the press to operate without government interference.

©83 Daytona Beach Morning Journal
BEATTE

"I propose we reword the First Amendment and make it:
FREEDOM FROM THE PRESS."

3. According to the cartoonist, which value was most important to President Reagan?

   (1) freedom of the press
   (2) making money
   (3) power of the president
   (4) solving America's problems
   (5) human rights

4. Based on this cartoon, what value seems to be most important to the cartoonist?

   (1) freedom of the press
   (2) making money
   (3) power of the presidency
   (4) solving America's problems
   (5) human rights

The New England town meeting has been called the purest form of democracy. At the meetings, every voter has the opportunity to "stand up and be counted" on issues that are important to the town. Any group coming to town meeting has the chance to appeal to the voters by speaking directly to them. One town preservation society thought they had an issue that couldn't lose at town meeting. They wanted the town to buy an old farm and save the land for recreation and education. Everybody on the purchase committee wanted a chance to speak to the voters. By the fourth speaker, the voters were getting impatient.

Then a speaker opposed to the purchase argued that the farm cost too much to buy. He also pointed out that the society had not estimated the costs of developing the land as a park or education center. How were the taxpayers to know what this purchase would cost in the long run?

Despite a poll of voters that showed them strongly in favor of saving open land, the proposed purchase of the farm was badly defeated.

5. What value of the voters did the town preservation society try to appeal to?
   (1) the need for efficiency
   (2) conservation of open land
   (3) the desire for lower taxes
   (4) the importance of communication
   (5) the spirit of fair play

6. The town preservation society was unsuccessful because
   (1) voters did not share the society's feeling about the importance of saving open land
   (2) voters wanted to lower their taxes
   (3) the purchase would not actually conserve any open land
   (4) voters were against increasing the recreational and educational resources of the town
   (5) voters were more concerned about the long-range costs than about conserving the land

Answers start on page 209.

PROPAGANDA

PROPAGANDA IN DAILY LIFE

Propaganda presents a person, a product, or an idea as good or bad. Its purpose is to convince you. You see examples of propaganda every day. The most common example of propaganda is advertising. Does the following example look familiar?

NEW MEDICAL BREAKTHROUGH!!!

Lose up to 50 Pounds Without Dieting
EAT ALL YOUR FAVORITE FOODS AND STILL LOSE WEIGHT

All of us have seen these kinds of ads before. They pull at our emotions and desires. They tell us that we can look great without having to do any work for it. They tell only the good side of their products and leave out any possible harmful side effects. They are a form of propaganda.

Propaganda uses information to convince a reader. It uses ideas, facts, or accusations to help or hurt a cause. Because it tries to promote a single point of view, it is generally one-sided. Propaganda often distorts facts. Advertisers use a variety of propaganda techniques to convince us to buy their products. How is this advertiser trying to convince you to buy the product?

TRAIN YOUR VOICE FOR SUCCESS!

Never again will you be overanxious or fearful when meeting new people or speaking in public. You will be absolutely self-confident knowing that your voice can have the resonance of a James Earl Jones, the controlled charm of a Courtney Cox, the poise of a Peter Jennings, or the seductive power of a Julia Roberts!

Order Your Voice-Training Cassette Right Away!

▶ This ad tries to convince you to buy the cassette by claiming that
    (1) it can make you speak as well as some famous people
    (2) you can become a famous actor if you use it
    (3) most people you know have benefited from it already
    (4) people who use it get better jobs
    (5) you don't need to improve your public speaking skills

The correct answer is choice (1). This is an example of a very common propaganda technique, the "famous or respected person" technique. By using the names of famous people, the ad tries to get you to think that you'll learn the same techniques that have made these people so successful.

Other common propaganda techniques include:

- Glittering generalities—using vague positive words and images

  Our salon's *secret techniques* will bring out the *timeless beauty* in you. Our experts think *age and elegance* go hand in hand.

- Name calling—connecting a negative image to an idea, a product, a person, or a group

  Stop using *dirty, smelly, smoky* oil. Change to electric heat.

- Bandwagon—everybody is doing it

  Join the Pepsi *Generation*! Drink Pepsi Cola.

- Cardstacking—mentioning only the favorable facts and ignoring the negative facts

  Top Choice Chewing Tobacco gives you that *real tobacco flavor without smoke.* For real tobacco satisfaction, use Top Choice.

  (Not mentioned in the ad are the dangers of smokeless tobacco.)

EXERCISE 8: PROPAGANDA AND ADVERTISING

Directions: Answer the questions following each advertisement.

> Eat Chocorich, America's highest-quality candy.
> Only the finest chocolate and sugar are used in making Chocorich.

1. According to the ad, you should eat Chocorich because
   - (1) everybody eats Chocorich
   - (2) famous people eat Chocorich
   - (3) eating Chocorich will make you popular
   - (4) more people eat Chocorich than any other candy
   - (5) other candy makers use lower-quality chocolate and sugar

2. The ad gives only reasons why you *should* eat Chocorich. Can you think of a reason not to eat Chocorich?

_____

_____

> Only those who dare . . . truly live
> DRIVE A FERRARI

3. This ad would appeal to
   (1) children who like to play with Barbie dolls
   (2) large families looking for a good family car
   (3) someone who wanted to appear adventurous
   (4) a banker trying to establish a solid, respectable image
   (5) a struggling young couple looking for their first car

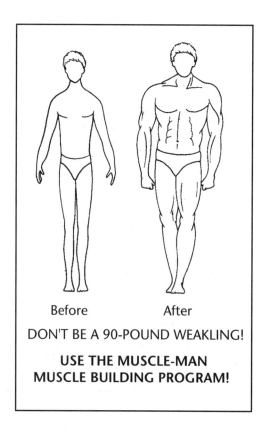

Before   After

DON'T BE A 90-POUND WEAKLING!

**USE THE MUSCLE-MAN
MUSCLE BUILDING PROGRAM!**

4. This ad appeals to people who believe that
   (1) attractive men have large muscles
   (2) it is a good idea to keep your weight down
   (3) it is important to be healthy
   (4) women like intelligent men
   (5) it is important to be considerate of others

5. Women will be attracted to this ad because
   (1) they look like the woman in the drawing
   (2) they are tired of the summer and want to look ahead to fall
   (3) they are looking for a bargain
   (4) they want to think of themselves as sophisticated
   (5) they do not want to attract attention to themselves

COME TO LESLIE'S!

We have sophisticated styles for fall.

Answers start on page 209.

POLITICAL PROPAGANDA

Propaganda has been used frequently in the political world. A lot of political propaganda consists of advertisements for political candidates. In addition, governments and political candidates use propaganda to convince people to support a cause. Political propaganda is also used to turn public opinion against other people or other countries, as in the following example.

> Englishmen cannot understand great ideas; they lack any real intelligence. They only care about material things and comforts.

▶ These ideas are an example of Italian propaganda at the beginning of World War II. What did the Italian government want its people to believe about the English?
   (1) The English were a dangerous enemy who must be feared.
   (2) The English were evil people who wanted to destroy the world.
   (3) The English were small-minded and could be defeated easily.
   (4) The English had a powerful economy that had to be destroyed.
   (5) The English were a noble people who should be copied.

The correct answer is choice (3). The writer says that the English lacked real intelligence. The Italian government insulted the English so that the Italian people would be more supportive of the war against the English.

EXERCISE 9: POLITICAL PROPAGANDA

Directions: Answer the questions following each passage or illustration.

> Following a disastrous defeat of the Germans by the Soviets at Stalingrad, Goebbels, Hitler's propaganda chief, spoke to the German people. He said that the 300,000 Germans killed in the battle were all heroes. They had slowed down six Soviet armies, which otherwise would be rampaging toward Germany. He claimed that the Germans had been "purified" by the defeat at Stalingrad. It had given them the new strength they required for victory.

1. List two reasons that, according to Goebbels, the defeat at Stalingrad was good for the Germans.

   _____

   _____

2. Why would Goebbels have described the terrible outcome of the Battle of Stalingrad as he did?

   (1) He believed that military defeats were good for the German spirit.
   (2) He thought the Russians might retreat.
   (3) He wanted the Americans and British to break their alliance with the USSR.
   (4) He didn't want people to realize what a disaster it was.
   (5) He wanted Germany to surrender to the Russians.

INTEREST IN HOLISTIC HEALING SKYROCKETS!

Americans nationwide are choosing holistic medicine over traditional treatment.

You too can experience the benefits of holistic healing!

---

3. According to this advertisement, you should try holistic medical treatment because

   (1) it works faster than traditional medical treatments
   (2) everybody is trying holistic medicine
   (3) traditional drugs have unhealthy side effects
   (4) a lot of research has gone into the development of holistic medicine
   (5) holistic medicines are much cheaper than other treatments

Source: *Propaganda, The Art of Persuasion: World War II* by Anthony Rhodes and Richard Ewart. Copyright 1983, Chelsea House Publishers, New York.

In English, this poster says "Benito Mussolini loves children very much. The children of Italy love the Duce very much. Long live the Duce. I salute the Duce: To us!"

4. This poster implies that the Italian people should support Mussolini because

(1) he is a great military leader
(2) he has lived a long time
(3) everybody in Italy is related to him
(4) he is a beloved father figure
(5) the enemies of Italy want him defeated

Answers start on page 209.

EXERCISE 10: CHAPTER REVIEW

Directions: Study each passage or picture, then answer the questions that follow.

1. This advertisement is trying to convince you that you should use Sauce Royale because

    (1) it is the best-tasting sauce
    (2) it is the healthiest sauce
    (3) it was made for a king
    (4) it was made by a famous chef
    (5) it is cheaper than other sauces

Questions 2–3 are based on the following map.

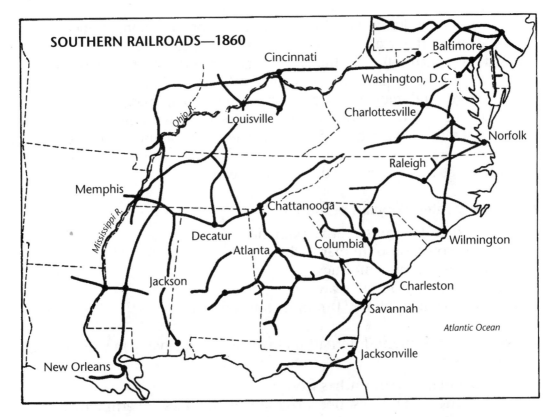

SOUTHERN RAILROADS—1860

2. According to the map, in 1860 it was impossible to travel by train from

   (1) Jackson to New Orleans
   (2) Atlanta to Columbia
   (3) Atlanta to Chattanooga
   (4) Raleigh to Charlottesville
   (5) Jacksonville to Savannah

3. There is enough information on the map to determine that

   (1) the North would win the Civil War by using the rail system to transport the troops
   (2) Atlanta was the largest city in the South because it was an important railroad junction
   (3) Savannah was the main shipping port for cotton because all cotton grown across the South could be shipped there by train
   (4) the western frontier could not be reached from the South by train
   (5) the South was mostly farmland and, therefore, did not need an extensive rail network

Questions 4–5 are based on the following passage.

> Amnesty International is a very special organization. It does not support any one form of government or economic system. It does watch out for human rights throughout the world, working on thousands of cases of political imprisonment, torture, and murder. As a result of this work, many people put into prison or tortured for their beliefs have been freed. Governments have been pressured to end their abuse of people who disagree with them. In recognition of its work, Amnesty International was awarded the Nobel Peace Prize.

4. Amnesty International's purpose is
   (1) the defeat of conservative politicians
   (2) the protection of human rights
   (3) the growth of democracy
   (4) the winning of major awards
   (5) the raising of money through contributions

5. To decide if Amnesty International has been effective, you would want to know
   (1) how many awards it has won
   (2) whether it has the support of the United States government
   (3) if it has helped make governments more respectful of human rights
   (4) whether it has fought against imperialism
   (5) whether it has been able to raise more money than other human rights groups

Questions 6–7 are based on the following passage.

The United Nations was founded after World War II to help nations solve their differences peacefully. While there has not been another world war, the past fifty years have been far from peaceful. For example, in the 1950s, the United Nations sent troops to fight in the Korean War. In addition, there was almost constant war in Southeast Asia and the Middle East for over half a century. And, even though the United Nations sent peacekeeping forces to the Balkans, horrible ethnic wars continued to rage.

Both the Security Council and the General Assembly of the United Nations were supposed to be places where nations could talk about their differences and solve them without violence. Unfortunately, nations have used these forums to attack each other verbally rather than to settle disputes.

6. From the passage, it is clear that

    (1) the United Nations has failed and should be abolished
    (2) the United Nations should be given more money
    (3) the United Nations has promoted war rather than prevented it
    (4) the United Nations still needs to develop ways to solve disputes peacefully
    (5) the United Nations should follow American foreign policy

7. A guiding principle of the United Nations is

    (1) only the strong survive
    (2) the meek shall inherit the earth
    (3) if you have the votes, you have the power
    (4) people should be free to live as they choose
    (5) conflicts should be settled peacefully

Background clues: On the July 4th weekend in 1986, there was a huge celebration of the 100th anniversary of the Statue of Liberty.

'OK, FIREBOATS—ON MY SIGNAL, WET THE T-SHIRT!'

8. According to the cartoonist, the celebration emphasized

    (1) the value of liberty
    (2) the dignity of the American people
    (3) tasteless commercialism
    (4) the importance of historical statues
    (5) the importance of immigrants to the United States

KEEP AMERICA STRONG!

VOTE FOR VITO AMORELLI FOR U.S. CONGRESS

9. As a voter, what reasonable response might you make to this ad?

    (1) voting for Vito because you want America to be strong
    (2) voting against Vito because you want America to be weak
    (3) not voting at all because it does not matter who is elected
    (4) finding out how Vito proposes to keep America strong
    (5) running for Congress yourself

10. "Equal pay for equal work" has become a rallying cry for women's groups. On the average, women are paid only two-thirds of what a man receives for either the same job or a job of equal difficulty and responsibility. What might be a good reason for a particular man to be paid more than a particular woman for a similar job?

    (1) He needs to be paid more because he must support a family.
    (2) Men are more important than women.
    (3) He has more years of experience than the woman.
    (4) He must save for retirement.
    (5) His pride would be hurt if a woman made as much as he.

11. Bill needs to buy a new pair of work gloves. He has to decide whether to buy the Powergrip brand or the Workingman brand. Which of the following is a good reason to buy the Powergrip brand glove?

    (1) It is a more durable and comfortable glove.
    (2) Robert Redford endorsed Powergrip gloves.
    (3) More people buy Powergrip than Workingman.
    (4) Bill's neighbor works for the company that makes Powergrip gloves.
    (5) Powergrip gloves cost more than Workingman gloves.

Answers start on page 210.

CHAPTER REVIEW EVALUATION CHART

Skill	Question Numbers*	Review Pages	Number Correct
Enough Information	2, 3	142–145	_____/2
Using Relevant Information	5, 6	146–149	_____/2
Errors in Reasoning	10, 11	149–153	_____/2
Recognizing Values	4, 7, **8**	154–157	_____/3
Propaganda	**1**, 9	158–163	_____/2

*Question numbers in **dark type** are based on illustrations.

Your score: _____ out of 11

Passing score: 8 out of 11

CHAPTER 6

APPLYING INFORMATION IN SOCIAL STUDIES

Your grandmother just had a heart attack and has been rushed to the hospital in a city over a thousand miles from where you live. You want to get there as soon as possible so that you can be with her. What form of transportation would you take?

You would probably go by airplane rather than by car, bus, or train. And you wouldn't even consider riding a bicycle or walking. By deciding to take a plane, you would be applying your knowledge of different types of transportation to your own needs.

WHAT IS APPLICATION?

Every day, you put the skills and information you have learned in your life to work for you in different situations. In this chapter, you will be applying information in a passage to new situations, just as you applied your knowledge of transportation to the situation described above. You will also study practical applications of information on maps, charts, and graphs, such as using information on a road map.

APPLYING INFORMATION IN EVERYDAY LIFE

Often you read or hear information you can apply to your daily needs. You are always picking up information and using it. For example, what do you think you might do to protect yourself or others if you read the following article in your daily newspaper?

Tylenol Tragedy

Police reported that five people in the Chicago area have died from taking Tylenol capsules laced with cyanide. Authorities say that the killer opened the capsules and added the cyanide. The bottles were then resealed and placed on store shelves. At this time the police have no suspects.

▶ What would you do? _____

_____

You might have done several things. First, you would probably throw away any Tylenol capsules you had. You also wouldn't buy any more until you were sure the capsules were safe. You also might think of warning other people, especially your family, of the danger of taking Tylenol capsules.

By responding to the article, you would have applied the information that Tylenol capsules are dangerous. In the following exercise, you'll practice this skill.

EXERCISE 1: APPLYING INFORMATION IN EVERYDAY LIFE

Directions: Read each passage, then choose the correct answer for each question that follows.

Regular exercise is more effective than dieting in helping people lose weight. A recent survey found that people who exercised for at least fifteen minutes at least three times per week were able to lose more weight than people using popular weight-loss diets. In a follow-up survey of the same people six months later, most exercisers had maintained their weight loss, while almost half the dieters had already regained what they had lost.

1. Earl wants to lose twenty pounds. Based on the information in the passage, what would be the best way for him to lose the weight and keep it off?

   (1) take diet pills and consume fewer calories
   (2) skip lunch every day
   (3) try a liquid diet
   (4) play tennis or basketball every weekend
   (5) walk briskly three miles at least three times a week

Automation has transformed the modern office. Computers have replaced the typewriter, and phone systems now allow people to conduct conference calls instead of face-to-face meetings. Many executives use tape recorders instead of dictating to a secretary who takes shorthand. In addition, large amounts of information are stored in databases instead of in file cabinets, and spreadsheet programs have replaced bookkeepers' ledgers. Offices can even send information from their computers to computers in other offices through electronic mail. With all these changes, employers' greatest need now is for people trained to use this new equipment.

2. Karl, who wants to find work in an office, read the previous passage in a brochure on career opportunities. Based on the passage, to help him find and keep a job, he should

   (1) learn to repair electronic equipment
   (2) take a course in shorthand, since stenographers are becoming very rare
   (3) work hard to increase his typing accuracy
   (4) get training in computer use in business offices
   (5) buy a newspaper and apply for jobs that sound interesting

Answers start on page 210.

APPLYING INFORMATION IN A PASSAGE

In social studies, you are often asked to apply information you read in a passage to answer a question or solve a problem. In the following example, you have a passage to read and then some choices to make. Apply the information in the passage to help you make the choices.

One hundred fifty years ago, farmers had to make the most of what they had. Typical farm families grew their own food. They also had a variety of farm animals, perhaps including cows, horses, pigs, and sheep. Their everyday clothes might be made from materials grown on the farm, such as wool, leather, cotton, and other fibers. Their homes were made from materials they could gather—wood, stones, even earth.

However, a farm family could not provide for all its needs. Plows, tools, nails, and other metal items were made by a blacksmith. Bowls and plates were made by a potter or imported. Glass windows, storage barrels, and wagon wheels were other items that a farmer had to purchase.

Put a *P* in front of those items that a farm family could *produce* on its farm. Put a *B* in front of those items that a farm family had to *buy*.

_____ 1. wooden spoons

_____ 2. milk

_____ 3. horseshoes

_____ 4. corn

_____ 5. tin lantern

You should have put a *P* in front of 1, 2, and 4. The farm family could carve wooden spoons, get milk from its own cow, and grow corn. You should have put a *B* in front of 3 and 5, horseshoes and a tin lantern. These would have to be bought from someone who could work metal.

EXERCISE 2: APPLYING INFORMATION IN A PASSAGE

Directions: Read each passage carefully, then answer the questions that follow.

A variety of government agencies provide services to people who need help. The Department of Health and Human Services provides some benefits, including Aid to Families with Dependent Children. Rehabilitation Services help people with handicapping conditions get the special programs and services they need. The Federal Council on Aging is an agency that provides the elderly with a variety of resources.

Following are descriptions of some people and the type of assistance they need. In the blank, mark the agency each should go to for help—*H* for Department of Health and Human Services, *R* for Rehabilitation Services, and *A* for the Federal Council on Aging.

_____ 1. A woman with two small children has been abandoned by her husband and has no job.

_____ 2. A seventy-one-year-old woman is lonely and wants to get out and spend time with other people.

_____ 3. A deaf man wants training in order to work with computers.

_____ 4. A family of four does not have enough money to buy food and clothing.

The development of the American West is limited by a shortage of water. Farmers, industry, residents, and recreational facilities all compete for water. In the future, communities will have to decide how to use their limited water supply. Will they use their water to grow more crops, to run more factories, to provide for a larger population and more homes, or to expand resorts and recreational facilities?

The city of Kerr has decided that its water will be put to best use for new homes and recreational development. The city is attractive to retired people as well as to tourists. The city council feels that construction of new homes, parks, and resorts will keep Kerr's economy strong.

Under this policy, which of the following requests for water access should the city approve? Write *yes* next to the projects the city *should* approve under the policy. Write *no* next to the projects the city should *not* approve.

_____ 5. An oil company wants to build a processing plant near Kerr and wants access to the city's water supply.

_____ 6. St. Mary's Hospital wants to build a new, larger facility to better meet the needs of the growing elderly population.

_____ 7. A chain of amusement parks wants to build a theme park outside Kerr and wants access to the city's water supply.

_____ 8. A farmer wants to buy a large piece of unirrigated land next to his farm. He wants permission to extend his watering system to the unirrigated land.

Answers start on page 210.

APPLYING INFORMATION ON A MAP

You can apply the information contained on all kinds of maps to real situations and decisions. Maps that you might come across in your everyday life include road maps, subway maps, and weather maps.

One of the most common ways that you might use a map is for deciding how to get from one place to another. For example, when you are trying to figure out a driving route, you look for the most direct route, the one that is closest to a straight line between the two places.

▶ You are a resident of Denver, Colorado. You want to drive to Los Angeles. Based on the interstate map on the next page, describe the shortest route you should take.

_____

First find Denver and Los Angeles on the map. Then find the route that is closest to a straight line. You should have taken Route 70 west to Route 15 south to Route 10 west.

INTERSTATE ROAD MAP—WESTERN UNITED STATES

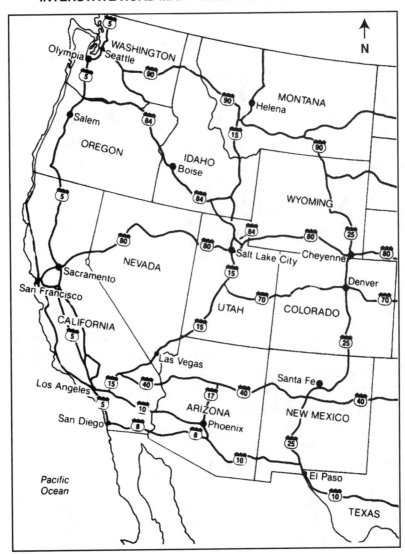

EXERCISE 3: APPLYING MAP SKILLS

Directions: Use information from the maps to answer the following questions. *Questions 1–2* are based on the interstate road map above.

1. You live in Olympia, Washington, and want to visit your brother in Cheyenne, Wyoming. What is the most direct route you could take?

   _____

   _____

2. You live in San Diego and want to travel to El Paso to see a rodeo. What is the shortest route you could take?

   _____

   _____

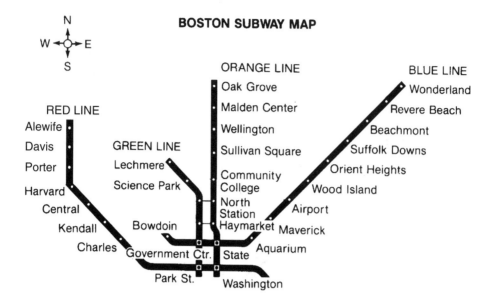

BOSTON SUBWAY MAP

3. How do you get from the airport to North Station on the Boston subway?

   (1) Take the Orange Line south to State and change to the Blue Line.
   (2) Take the Blue Line southwest to State and change to the Red Line going northwest.
   (3) Take the Orange Line south to Washington and change to the Blue Line going northwest.
   (4) Take the Blue Line southwest to State and change to the Orange Line going north.
   (5) Take the Blue Line southwest.

4. A student at Harvard University wants to visit the Science Museum at Science Park. How would she get there by subway?

   (1) Take the Red Line southeast.
   (2) Take the Green Line north.
   (3) Take the Red Line southeast to Park St. and change to the Green Line going north.
   (4) Take the Blue Line southwest to Government Center and change to the Green Line going north.
   (5) Take the Red Line southeast to Park St. and change to the Orange Line going north.

Answers start on page 210.

APPLYING DATA ON CHARTS AND GRAPHS

In social studies, you will often be asked to apply the information on charts and graphs when you need to solve a problem. In the following example, apply the information on the bar graph to figure out what the board of education's long-range plan should be. The Mozlin Board of Education is planning ahead three years for its high school building and teachers.

STUDENT POPULATION, MOZLIN PUBLIC SCHOOL

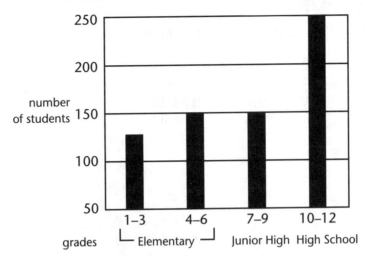

1. How many students are there now in grades 10–12? _____

2. How many students are there now in grades 7–9? _____

3. In three years, will the student body of the Mozlin High School have

   increased, decreased, or remained about the same? _____

4. Given the information on the bar graph, which of the following should the board of education plan to do within three years?

   (1) hire more high school teachers
   (2) build a second high school
   (3) close the high school, because there won't be any students
   (4) reduce the number of high school teachers
   (5) send overflow students to other schools

1. There are 250 students. Find grades 10–12 on the horizontal axis. Go to the top of the bar above 10–12 and read the number of students from the vertical axis.

2. There are 150 students. Find grades 7–9 on the horizontal axis and read the height of the bar.

3. The student body in the high school will decrease. Compare the top of the 7–9 bar with the top of the 10–12 bar. In three years the current junior high students (7–9) will be in high school. That means that in three years there will be about 150 students in the high school, many fewer than the 250 there now.

4. The correct answer is choice (4), *reduce the number of high school teachers.* Since there will be fewer students, fewer teachers will be needed. Choices (1), (2), and (5) are incorrect because there will be fewer students. The school should not close, choice (3), since there will still be students.

EXERCISE 4: APPLYING INFORMATION ON CHARTS AND GRAPHS

Directions: Use the information from each chart or graph to answer the questions.

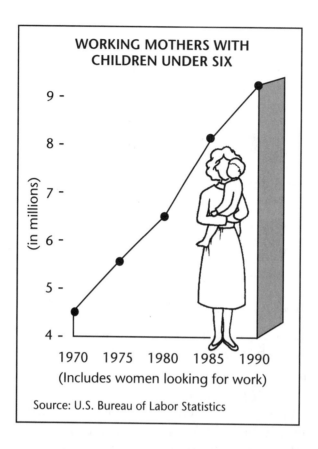

WORKING MOTHERS WITH CHILDREN UNDER SIX

(in millions)

1970 1975 1980 1985 1990

(Includes women looking for work)

Source: U.S. Bureau of Labor Statistics

1. What change does the graph show taking place between 1970 and 1990?

   (1) More women with children under six years of age decided to stay home.
   (2) There are fewer women with children under six.
   (3) The number of working mothers with children under six has more than doubled.
   (4) Working mothers have learned more about health care for children under six.
   (5) The number of working mothers with children under six has stabilized.

2. Based on this information, a new company that wanted to attract young women into its work force might consider offering

   (1) security guards at night in areas where women work
   (2) Club Med vacations
   (3) on-site day-care facilities
   (4) on-site athletic facilities
   (5) weekly social events in the evenings

CONSUMER REPORTER TELEPHONE COMPARISON

Phone	Price	Durability	Ease of Use
Sunbrand SlimPhone	$55	excellent	poor
Blackdeck Desktop	$75	good	excellent
Radio House Cordless	$85	fair	poor
HomePhone Basic	$25	fair	good

3. Mary is buying a phone for her elderly father, whose hands are stiffened by arthritis. Which phone should she choose?

_____

4. Leonard is buying a phone for the kitchen in his home. The phone will be in constant use by his family of six, including his four teenaged children. Which phone should he choose?

_____

5. Lydia has just moved out of her parents' home. She has only a few hundred dollars saved to furnish her apartment. Her job requires that she have a phone at home. Which phone should she choose?

_____

Answers start on page 210.

EXERCISE 5: CHAPTER REVIEW

Directions: Answer the questions following each passage or illustration.

Questions 1–2 are based on the following map.

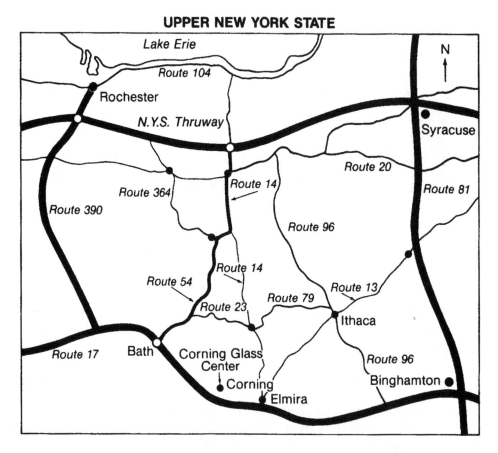

UPPER NEW YORK STATE

1. You live in Rochester and want to visit the Corning Glass Center in
    Corning. What is the most direct route you could take?
    (1) Route 390 south to NYS Thruway, east to Route 14, south to
    Route 17 west
    (2) Route 390 south to NYS Thruway, east to Route 14, south to
    Route 54, south to Route 17 east
    (3) Route 104 east to Route 14, south to Route 17 west
    (4) Route 390 south to NYS Thruway, east to Route 81, south to
    Route 17 west
    (5) Route 390 south to Route 17 east

2. The shortest route from the city of Syracuse to the town of Bath is
    (1) NYS Thruway west to Route 14, south to Route 17 west
    (2) NYS Thruway west to Route 14, south to Route 54 south
    (3) NYS Thruway west to Route 390, south to Route 17 east
    (4) Route 81 south to Route 17 west
    (5) Route 81 south to Route 13, south to Route 17 west

Questions 3–4 are based on the following chart.

COMPACT CAR COMPARISON CHART			
	Price	**Gas Mileage**	**Repair Record**
Hyundai Splash	$12,500	25 city 45 highway	poor
Geo Elite	$12,800	27 city 50 highway	better than average
Honda Attractiva	$13,900	30 city 52 highway	better than average
Mazda Prestige	$14,500	23 city 45 highway	average
Nissan Esprit	$14,800	28 city 50 highway	average

3. Mario is a traveling salesman in a rural area. He drives mostly on highways and needs a very reliable car. Which car from the chart above should he buy?

   (1) Hyundai Splash
   (2) Geo Elite
   (3) Honda Attractiva
   (4) Mazda Prestige
   (5) Nissan Esprit

4. Libby cannot afford to pay more than $13,000 for a car. In addition, she wants to buy a car that will have low repair costs. Which car from the chart above should she buy?

   (1) Hyundai Splash
   (2) Geo Elite
   (3) Honda Attractiva
   (4) Mazda Prestige
   (5) Nissan Esprit

Question 5 is based on the following paragraph.

> In order to ensure a stable food supply for the United States, the U.S. government has an extensive farm support program. This program pays farmers not to plant some of their fields, since we don't need the food right now. These fields are not given up for other uses because they could be needed to produce food in the future. These idle fields could be planted to respond to a national food emergency, such as failure of an important crop because of major drought or disease.

5. Based on the passage, the federal government should *not* pay farmers to preserve unplanted tobacco fields because
   (1) tobacco farmers do not practice sound farm management
   (2) enough tobacco is being produced
   (3) cigarettes have been shown to cause cancer
   (4) tobacco would not be needed in a national food emergency
   (5) the tobacco lobby in Washington has been weakened by antismoking campaigns

Questions 6–7 are based on the following passage.

> Teenagers today seem angry, and they lack direction. They often express their frustrations through antisocial, even violent, acts such as breaking windows, spray painting profanity on walls, or stealing cars. Poor children are not the only ones who commit these crimes. These things happen in wealthy suburbs as well.
> Because rich teens get in trouble just as deprived teens do, we cannot blame their crimes on their not having money or possessions they want. Instead, we must realize that these young people have almost nothing useful or important to do. They have a lot of energy to use up. If they have no positive outlet for their energy, it will come out in a destructive way.

6. The author of this passage feels that teenagers commit crimes because
   (1) they want money
   (2) they don't have their own cars
   (3) they have nothing useful to do
   (4) they have no outlet for their artistic urges
   (5) they don't know any better